U. Mc. g. A.

Feb 22, 2005

re read Dec 11-13-2012

CROSSING HIGHBRIDGE

 Irish Studies

Sanford Sternlicht, *Series Editor*

Crossing HIGHBRIDGE

A MEMOIR OF IRISH AMERICA

Maureen Waters

 SYRACUSE UNIVERSITY PRESS

First edition 2001
01   02   03   04   05   06   6   5   4   3   2   1

Although this book is a memoir, some names have been changed to protect the
privacy of those individuals.

The paper used in this publication meets the minimum requirements of American National
Standard for Information Sciences—Permanence of Paper for Printed Library Materials, ANSI
Z39.48-1984.∞™

Library of Congress Cataloging-in-Publication Data

Waters, Maureen, 1939–
    Crossing Highbridge : a memoir of Irish America / Maureen Waters.—1st ed.
        p. cm. — (Irish studies)
    ISBN 0-8156-0682-6 (alk. paper)
        1. Waters, Maureen, 1939—Childhood and youth. 2. Irish American women—New
    York (State)—New York—Biography. 3. Irish Americans—New York (State)—New
York—Biography. 4. Catholic women—New York (State)—New York—Biography. 5.
Catholics—New York (State)—New York—Biography. 6. Bronx (New York,
N.Y.)—Biography. 7. Bronx (New York, N.Y.)—Social life and customs—20th century. 8.
New York (N.Y.)—Biography. 9. New York (N.Y.)—Social life and customs—20th century. I.
Title. II. Irish studies (Syracuse, N.Y.)
F128.68.B8 W38 2000
974.7'10049162073—dc21   00-046389

Manufactured in the United States of America

To David, for loving intervention

Maureen Waters is professor of English at Queens College. She is the author of *The Comic Irishman* and coeditor of *Lady Gregory: Selected Writings*. Her essays and reviews appear in *Yeats: An Annual of Critical and Textual Studies*, *Éire-Ireland*, *Études Irlandaises*, the *Canadian Journal of Irish Studies*, the *Irish Literary Supplement*, and the *Irish University Review*. In 1998, the Honor Society of Queens College presented her with a golden apple as Teacher of the Year.

CONTENTS

ILLUSTRATIONS

PREFACE

This book was prompted by the tragic loss of a son, who had broken away from the family. Visiting Chicago, where he died in 1993, led me to remember events much further back in time and to realize how much we had all been affected by the vagaries of history. My immigrating parents came of age during the Irish revolution and civil war and were deeply scarred by that experience. My sister and I were brought up, not as Roman Catholics, but as Irish ones, with all the extremes of practice and belief the term implies. The voices of our childhood were melancholy, cantankerous, and humorous all at once. The play of wit was a mode of survival and communication, as was the habit of storytelling. I have included in the Appendix a story by my father, who most influenced me, in order to illustrate the long reach of his memories. To some extent writing this down has become a means of recovery as well as a tribute to the vitality and courage of those who are gone.

ACKNOWLEDGMENTS

J want to thank those who advised and encouraged me in writing this book, particularly Agnes Waters, Nora Ruane, Ruth Sartisky, Susan and Tom Cahill, Lucy McDiarmid, Carol and Charles Molesworth, Charles Fanning, John Wright, Fred Kaplan, Sandra Siegel, Hazel Weinberg, and David Kleinbard. For help in researching Bronx history, I want to express appreciation to Janet Munch, Special Collections, Lehman College, and to the staff of the Highbridge Library and the Bronx County Historical Society. For permission to quote "Anniversary" in its entirety, I thank David Kleinbard. I want to acknowledge the *Crab Orchard Review*, *The Irish Literary Supplement*, *New York Irish History*, and *Book Press* in which portions of *Crossing Highbridge* initially appeared. Special thanks are due also to the editorial staff at Syracuse University Press and to Dolores Beckerman and Julie Grant for preparing the manuscript.

CROSSING HIGHBRIDGE

Maureen, about five years old, and her sister, Agnes.
Franz Sigel Park, the Bronx. Courtesy of the author.

BRIAN PATRICK

Chicago, December 1995

I am attending a meeting of the Modern Language Association at
the Hyatt Regency, a mammoth hotel whose twin glass towers
enclose two thousand rooms. Mine is located in a corner of the West
Tower from which I travel eastward across a skyway festooned with
Christmas lights. Or I plunge underground via two escalators to the corridor which leads through a labyrinth of conference rooms, display areas,
and shops. The books are down there. I have a map in hand to guide me,
and I've learned to read the pastel display charts signaling the intercon-
necting planes and corridors of this hotel. There are a lot of dead ends.

But it's easy to locate the sparkling dome in the East Tower, where a
three-story holiday extravaganza is mounted. Here, professors and
would-be professors of language and literature meet for drinks amid ice
floes over which polar bears in top hats and red mufflers and troops of
tiny penguins disport themselves. Along the rectangular border of this
enclave, forty-foot-tall penguins gaily rotate among palm trees. Music is
piped in. Neon stars twinkle above and a Hyatt Regency waterfall twin-
kles below. Incongruous, to say the least. The New York press, citing
some of our trendier topics of discussion, might say the form is the con-
tent: Disneyland is the perfect site for the revels of postcolonialism, fem-
inism, poststructuralism, et al. The Chicago press is gentler, noting with
interest the attribution to Shakespeare of a funeral elegy, on the basis of
computerized analysis.

In the conference area the mood is different. The holiday music and
the glitz are minimally distracting. I'm here myself to chair a panel on
contemporary Irish fiction and to meet other scholars in my field, which

is Irish studies. I am a tenured professor at Queens College of the City University of New York, fortunate in this respect. Many of the conferees whom I meet this year are women and men looking for jobs or anxious to hold on to the ones they have. They have come to Chicago to be interviewed, to give and listen to papers, to meet publishers, to network. From my fourth-floor window, I watch them in the cold morning light walking toward the opening session, briefcases in hand, bent slightly forward with a certain stiffness about the knees. A certain stiffening of the psyche, perhaps. Lee, my surviving son, a Yale Ph.D., is among them.

Three years ago Brian, my younger son, died in this city—an accidental death, the coroner said. For six days he lay unclaimed in the Cook County morgue. He went out on New Year's Eve and never came back. And although we frantically contacted city officials and friends all over Chicago, no one could give us any information. For six days we didn't know what had happened to him. As time went by I actually began to feel easier. He was impulsive. He might be on his way home from Chicago. At any minute he might be at the door.

The fact is that he died in a house on Lombard Street, a house boarded up now because of a fire. It is nowhere near Chicago's fabled Golden Mile. I like to imagine it as belonging to Carl Sandburg's Chicago, "City of the Big Shoulders . . . Tool Maker, Stacker of Wheat." An anachronism, of course, but Brian was a workingman.

On another map, provided by the Hyatt Regency, I recognize a few local names: Lakewood Drive, Cook County, names printed on official documents that sealed his disappearance. I can't easily determine the location of these places in relation to my own. From the window of my tower, there is no view of the inner city or the nearby lake. I seem to be surrounded by glass structures, perpetually lighted from within, weirdly distorting the shapes of passing walkers and automobiles.

At a certain slant of light in the frosty afternoon, I am lulled into a sense that nothing is happening at all, that there has been no change. My room seems suspended in a vacuum of blue light; there is no noise in the corridor; no sound penetrates from the plaza below. This is one aspect of grief: the icy disconnectedness of things.

And what would I find on Lombard Street? His ghost, perhaps, lingering to offer an explanation. Or the ultimate nausea, vomiting up the tumor of grief in tears, mucus, rage.

It is strange to be writing this down, to be thinking about syntax and the placing of words on paper. But writing is my training and my heritage. It is the thing that soothes, that enables me to get from day to day, to present a face to the world. There are mounds of paper in my study in New York, stuffed into drawers and closets, piled on the desk. The words accumulate. I go back to the beginning again and again.

Writing encourages clarity, helping one to understand the experience one has lived through, which is what I always tell my students. And that is usually the result if one writes honestly. But sometimes all one can do is bear witness, to say this happened, I loved this one, and now he is gone. There are connections, there are reasons one will never know.

When my father died, he left a memoir of his youth in Ireland and his first years struggling to find work in New York City during the Depression. Reading that memoir, I hear distinctly the rich inflections of his voice. All I have from Brian are a few letters, a few sketches, drawings, cartoons. They are infused with optimism; the colors are bright and fresh; the sun is coming up; flowers bloom.

There is a poem by John Donne, "The Relique," which meditates on a trace of beauty evocative even in death. "the bracelet of bright hair about the bone." But there is no trace of Brian's bright red hair. He was cremated so that his remains could be interred with those of his grandparents. It was an agonizing decision. I felt that I was annihilating him all over again—a crazy notion that ties in with Catholic practice, a respect for the body, traditionally left intact, untouched as a sign of hope in resurrection. A sign of hope. I feared I was destroying his chances. The traveling people in Ireland, however, believe that burning releases the soul, lets it go free. There is some comfort in that thought, but only some; it is hard to fit what actually happened to any ritual.

For a long time you don't believe it's true. And because I never saw him in death, there are moments when I am still convinced that he's out there somewhere, just crossing the horizon, expectant, buoyant as ever. All that came back to me were official papers. Certificates of death, an autopsy report, a police report listing items of his clothing, distinguishing physical marks, the contents of his stomach. His wallet was missing, so they were unable to identify him until Nancy, his dear, frantic Nancy, went to the morgue on January 6. The police called his brother, who called me. It could have been anyone.

How does one bear the death of a child? "The heart's needle" it was termed by an anonymous Irish poet. How does one go on living afterward, from year to year, knowing he is irretrievably lost? It would, I suppose, have been worse had he been younger, had he experienced less of life; he would have remained forever a beautiful, idealized child. Indeed, I keep thinking of him as younger and more vulnerable than he was, searching in memory for the responsive, amiable child in the face of the implacable man.

Brian was a mischievous child, who climbed out of his crib, climbed over the walls of the playground, up into the tallest trees. He invariably found whatever I was hiding on the top shelf of the kitchen cabinet. His was the first toe out in the morning and the most reluctant into bed at night. He was funny and fearless and inquisitive; attached to small animals and to his big brother, whom Brian taught to ride a two-wheeled bike. He came close to death more than once through accidents and through the respiratory infections which had killed children in earlier generations. But I always caught him in time, called the police, got him to an emergency room, sealed him in an oxygen tent.

Brian was not a child who died, but a difficult, thirty-three-year-old man who would not or could not settle down in one place or hold a steady job. He rejected the world he grew up in, tattooed the biceps on both arms, dressed in shabby black leather and a biker's cap. He was moody and impulsive, and he drank too much. But he was an affectionate, devoted husband to the woman he loved, a good father to Jeremiah, the son he adopted. They were the core of the life he was trying to create for himself.

A friend once said to me, "Don't worry, Maureen. There are no hippies over thirty. They finally wise up and come in out of the cold." There was comfort in that thought, and the signs were often promising. Brian was a skilled carpenter and lived well for a time with his family in New Hampshire. But then he lost his job, refused help, and slipped into a brutal downward spiral that lasted for nearly two years. He had just turned it around when he died. Another friend suggested it was the sort of thing that can happen to anyone at any time. A car can skid into a tree—or into an open field if you're lucky. He was in a lot of physical pain that night. He took the risk and hit the tree.

It did not surprise me that he had no identification papers. He had rejected his father's name, and he wouldn't accept mine either. He invented names, tried them on, built up a kind of legend for himself under a code name: Woodstock. Then simply Stock—basic, solid, nonspecific. The romantic sixties blending with hardworking, blue-collar toughness.

In traditional Irish society the grieving woman was thought to exist in an altered state which allowed her to mediate between the supernatural world and this one. When she cried out in rage or sorrow, no harm was attached to what she said. There was, moreover, a formal rhythmic pattern for the articulation of grief, known as the *caoine*. Suppressed by the clergy in modern times, it was a kind of chant in praise of the dead, which was taken up in antiphonal response by other women in the community. The chant, with its attendant ritual laughter, effected reconciliation between the living and the dead, enabling the departed to take his place among his ancestors in the other world.

I rarely speak of this death. I hug it to me, fold it inside my chest. I am not trying to be stoical or to spare anyone's feelings. It's a kind of prelogical impulse: Do not name the thing, and it will have no reality. There are days when I want to complain, to be openly depressed and truculent, to smash windows. Yet that would call attention to the very thing that must be disguised like a horrible wound that has begun to heal, if only on the surface. A sudden move and it ruptures, and I say something altogether crazy. I counter these impulses with schedules of papers due, classes to be taught, appointments to keep. My desk, indeed much of the house, is strewn with notes and memoranda. There are books half-read and newspapers and quite a list of calls to be made. American women are enjoined to maintain a sociable presence, and the pull of the social provides relief. The pattern is there, easy to observe, to follow. Let it pull me wherever it chooses. Time, everyone agrees, will help. I will begin to forget, to find new loves to cherish. My heart will mend.

One goes back to origins, thinking it will help one to find the answers or the turning points that led to the inevitable tragedy. One agonizes: If only I had done this or that, he would be alive now. There is even the notion of purification, of rites to be performed. In "The Swimmer," a short story by John Cheever, a man goes from one pool to another, following a water course through northern Westchester, swimming back to the house where he had been happy. The story suggests a desire for rebirth, for the chance to do it right the next time. There is even the suggestion that if he performs the ritual painstakingly, the events of dispersal, divorce, and breakdown will be eradicated. When he gets there finally in a cold driving rain, the house is boarded up.

Yes, the story embodies a persistent desire—childish, of course, heartbreaking, primitive—for a second chance. But how to find the right turning point? If only I had never married? But then my sons would not have been born. It is impossible to think of their never having lived at all. I've tried therapy. I've tried Prozac. They helped a great deal. But the sense of loss is as powerful as ever. There is no muffling it, and indeed I don't want to. It's one way of acknowledging the vitality of what is gone.

Though I've spent many fifty-minute hours trying to understand why Brian chose to live dangerously, taking risk after risk, the process was ultimately futile. I realized that driving the attempt to piece together cause and effect was a belief that I had far more power than I actually did for good or ill. Wasn't I the supermom who refused to get sick or collapse or ask anyone for help? Perhaps I am deluding myself again, but I don't think so. And at this point such scrutiny is meaningless. There are better ways to think about him and bring him back into the family story. In the end there was an accident with alcohol and drugs. I don't know the particulars and, even if I did, I wouldn't know how to interpret them. Brian was full of plans. He had a new job and money in his pocket. He was living with the woman and child he loved in a house on Greenbay Road in Chicago—a providential name and one he would have taken notice of.

In a sequence of poems titled *North,* Seamus Heaney imagines the Irish bog as a contrasting or answering myth to the prairie, which embodies the American myth of progress. He speaks of digging down through the boggy layers of history in an effort to understand how the people of Ulster became trapped in a cycle of violence. The immigrant to the United States, on the other hand, has glimpsed the prairie, if not as a symbol of progress, at least as one of hope. When I start digging, I am reaching for a stratum of solid bedrock. My early years of life corresponded with the years in which my immigrating family first settled in New York. It was a time of hope.

I am well aware of how memory shifts and fluctuates, and I know that one can't help reshaping the past even as one struggles to retrieve it. Yet I need to locate that first foothold on America, need to see it freshly defined like the contours of Celtic fortifications, which are visible in aerial photos from a great distance, invisible up close.

My parents were not wide-eyed optimists. They conveyed a sense of energy and commitment that had less to do with material progress than with some spiritual investment. Though we lived in a fourth-floor walk-up—a small apartment—we had a room with a view, an expanding horizon. We looked at bridges, trains, the river with its shifting lights, the open sky. One could sit there for hours, winter and summer, listening to voices in the street. We had a window on America. It belonged to us in all its vividness, with all the possibilities that lurked around the corner or on the other side of the bridge.

My mother's sisters, now in their seventies and eighties, were interviewed recently by an historian who was collecting data on Irish immigration. What they remembered most strongly was their pleasure in New York City. No matter that they worked as waitresses, that they had little money. They were delighted with their brave new world. Their eyes seemed to take in nothing that was ordinary. And they were not innocents, nor were they simply expressing relief in having escaped from the old country.

Perhaps that made the crucial difference in my childhood: the fact that the immigrant experience was so new. For us it was a momentous thing that one uncle had a car. We could ride through the northern and eastern reaches of the Bronx and Westchester, picnic in Van Cortland Park or in Pelham Bay, walk through fields of golden dragon lilies. Even coffee was something special, brewed in a glass percolator by that same uncle, who sold it for a living and whose car retained the rich odor of coffee throughout our Sunday afternoon drives. Coffee was exotic, flavored with cream, redolent of unimaginable treats to come. So as a child I absorbed a sense of newness twice over; whatever I looked at was framed by this immigrant perspective.

It took a while to understand how that mythical Irish bog had claims as well.

Maureen, Agnes, and their father, Daniel Waters.
Franz Sigel Park. Courtesy of the author.

BRONX IRISH

THE BRIDGE

It's no easy thing to locate the Bronx. From the Upper West Side of Manhattan, you have to find your way through congested streets and around roadblocks. Attempting to cross the Harlem River, you become tangled in the bowels of the George Washington Bridge. There is a sign for the Cross Bronx Expressway, but is there a sign for the Bronx? Not even visible until you have tunneled through to the border of Washington Heights, it is the borough to bypass rapidly on the way to somewhere else. On both sides of the expressway, it is a place of ruin, dilapidated or burned-out buildings, broken glass.

In 1987 I went back for the first time in twenty years. Turning off in the direction of University Avenue, I followed a scarred, wreckage-strewn route across the Washington Bridge to the Highbridge section in what was once designated the West Bronx. Along with everything else south of Fordham Road, it has been subsumed by the South Bronx, a term synonymous with the worst form of urban blight. The bridge itself, built in 1889 and noted for its ornamental ironwork, was visibly rotting; the twisted, burned hulk of an automobile straddled the entranceway on either side, while the rusted infrastructure was exposed through its entire length.

In the early nineteenth century, this was a farming area with apple and cherry orchards. The community of Highbridge sprang up in the 1830s and 1840s, peopled mainly by Irish immigrants who helped build the aqueduct to the south of the Washington Bridge. This Roman-style structure originally had fifteen high stone arches that allowed navigation upriver; hence, it was called the High Bridge. It was ready to pipe water from Croton Reservoir into Manhattan in 1842. A famous landmark in its day, the bridge was considered a major feat of engineering, remarkable for its views. On both sides pleasant wooded bluffs stretched northward toward Spuyten Duyvil (the Spitting Devil); downriver one could see MacComb's Dam and, beyond that, the thickets of Central Park. Among the sightseers in the 1840s was Edgar Allan Poe, who used to walk down from his home on Kingsbridge Road in the village of Fordham. On the Manhattan side, from 1872, water was stored in a Gothic high tower built of granite—not unlike an Irish stone tower—that stood at the summit of the hill. During the late nineteenth century, Highbridge was a resort with restaurants and parks, which attracted travelers brought by steamers up the Harlem River. In 1987 the landmark bridge, the oldest in the city, was a ruin barricaded by iron bars. The tower, struck by arson, appeared to have exploded in midair.

Since then there have been stirrings of renewal. The tower has been rebuilt, Highbridge Park is being replanted, the footbridge restored. But on the east side of the Harlem River little remains of my childhood world.

In the early 1940s when our family moved to Highbridge, there were strong traces of its nineteenth-century origins as well as handsome specimens of art deco buildings constructed in the 1930s. Highbridge did not have the elegance of the Grand Concourse or the handsome prosperity of Mosholu Parkway, but in the courtyard of the Noonan Plaza there were swans. That's probably what turned my head in the first place—that and the river view from our fourth-story walk-up on University Avenue.

Highbridge was mainly a working-class community, scrappy, opinionated, with Jewish and Irish residents, many of them recent immigrants with a nostalgia for the "old country" and an inclination to attach themselves to "the block." There were small shops and private homes, both shabby and genteel. Horse-drawn wagons came by with fresh fruits and vegetables, and a trolley line ran along Ogden Avenue, an original thoroughfare. Like much of the Bronx—Bronck's Land—Highbridge was dotted with parks, some of them such as Brown's Hill or Boscobel Park remnants of nineteenth-century estates. The area stretched out along one of the three ridges, shinbones of the Appalachian Mountains, which give the West Bronx its distinctive hilly terrain. In front of our apartment house, which stood above the High Bridge, steps led steeply down past the stone waterworks buildings toward the river. Rosebushes grew alongside those steps, and there were chickens in some backyards.

UNIVERSITY AVENUE

The life of the neighborhood spilled out into the street. In our apartment house, which has vanished completely, windows were open and doors stood ajar. Everyone was familiar. Families grew larger; four and five children were squeezed in together, but no one ever moved because the rent was cheap. We were accustomed to a rattling hum on all sides, the domestic quarrels upstairs and down. We knew which baby had colic, who had chicken pox, whose father had come home for dinner. We usually knew what he was eating, too. The corridors reeked of cooking: ham and cabbage, sausages, beef stew. There was little visiting between one small apartment and another. The women in housedresses leaned over the banisters or the windowsills to talk to neighbors or went outside, arranging themselves like a Mayo chorus along the stone fence across the street.

Our apartment house and those adjoining it were only five stories high, fitting the congenial scale of many European cities. In central and southern Highbridge, near Yankee Stadium, there were tall art deco buildings, which combined the exotic—Mayan and Aztec flourishes, twin towers, a waterfall—with a modern, recessed, geometric design, complete with elevators. In our part of town there were courtyards planted with trees and shrubs but an elevator was a rarity, so, whether we liked it or not, there was plenty of exercise, particularly on washdays when the roof was aswarm with flopping sheets and towels and swelling bloomers. I can still smell the tarry, irregular surface of Bronx rooftops and remember the vertigo I felt looking over the edge—like the edge of a subway platform—imagining that the whole thing might dip abruptly and I would be pitched into space.

Early on, I developed a sense that my footing was a trifle uncertain, subject to sudden shifts and dislocations. Irish girls, my father maintained, were awkward on their feet, like ducks or geese, perhaps, more at home in other spheres. The first sign of this enduring affliction occurred when I sprained an ankle on the steps of the Bronx Courthouse and was forced to resume a seat in the family stroller, a splendid large wicker stroller. Unlike the efficient aluminum matchsticks of today, it was a highly visible affair. Wheeled about for weeks, swathed in adhesive tape from knee to toe, I seethed with misery, fearing that the world would judge me, at age five, an overgrown baby.

Was it then I sensed how reluctantly an Irish family loosens its grip?

On University Avenue there were several older women living near us in mother-daughter combinations, who looked much the same to my child's eye. We saw them rarely but sensed them listening behind their doors as we came and went; the usual bombardment of neighborly sounds wasn't enough for them. Growing up, my sister, Agnes, and I felt surrounded by curious ears and eyes, by people who asserted their kinship and hence the right to know everything about us. We might as well have been living in an Irish village. No matter what time or with whom we arrived, there was an interested witness "on the fence" or behind a door. Mother made use of this circumstance to keep us in line: "What will the neighbors think?" "We don't want the neighbors to know." She remained aloof from the enterprising, gossipy inclinations of the community.

Downstairs lived the Dohertys, a family of five daughters, pink-cheeked and pretty with fair curly hair and cranky dispositions. There seemed always a smaller and a yet smaller one trailing down the stairs, struggling to keep up with the rest. They were a provoking lot, inclined to hold grudges and to be better than anyone else—regular whirling dervishes—at jumping rope. If you tackled one, in an attempt at justice, the whole tribe would be after you. The oldest, who regularly left Agnes's shins black and blue, shocked us all by joining the Sisters of Charity when she was fourteen. This was Peggy, who could name all the states in alphabetical order and tell you their capitals and a great deal more besides, if you gave her an opening.

Like most of the kids on the block, the Dohertys were intensely competitive at ball games, games with marbles and chalk, kick the can, red light-green light, potsie, as well as jumping rope. We played ball games obsessively against the stoop and along the walls of the buildings, box ball on the sidewalk, softball on the street with the boys jeering from the sideline. There was a fierce interest in coming out on top, holding out the longest, beating off all comers. Nobody played with dolls (at least not in public). What a strange group of girls we were, children of immigrants, fighting for a toehold in the promised land. Expected to be little angels at home and certainly at school; cramped up for hours in small spaces, we had energy to burn.

No one ever turned the other cheek except the one Jewish girl on our block. Marlene, the peacemaker, plump and hospitable, invited us all to her home, opting for rational discourse at the center of the daily squall. Actually I preferred peace myself and often maintained it, as I was one of the older kids. But I went in terror of two other girls—no bigger than myself, really, yet fully capable of leaving me dazed on the sidewalk. At twelve I struck a truce with the more combative one, a stout girl with eyes like prune pits, because we were both in love with the same handsome boy. When I married (someone else entirely), she attached herself to Mother, often carrying home packages for her from the store, and they would talk about the old days when we were kids together.

Agnes, younger, small of stature, but wonderfully outspoken, had a much harder time of it. Outnumbered by the usual bloodthirsty gang, she would race for the lobby of our building and frantically press our bell. This was my signal to drop everything and tear downstairs to rescue her. All I had to do was emerge ferociously in daylight, and the attackers took to their heels. One time I overreacted by chasing one brat, Margy Shannon, all the way back to her own apartment house and up five flights of stairs. At the top, just as I was reaching for her skinny red neck, her mother appeared—the very image of maternal wrath—and chased me down those same five flights and back up to my own door. There, fortunately, my own mother waited—a barrier between me and all harm, implacable in the teeth of the Shannons: "If I get my hands on that one . . ."

How nimble I was with my rickety ankles securely gripped by Woolworth's sneakers. How speedily I covered the blocks, dodging snowballs, rocks, stockings packed with flour on Halloween. When not on foot, I raced on skates, the key in perpetual motion on a chain around my neck (and worn secretly under my uniform at school). We played tag, flying down the steps of the park and around the stone waterworks across the street, on and off the sidewalks, defying fate and gravity, a terror to pedestrians.

The one signal that cleared the block, bringing instantaneous peace to the neighborhood, was the summons to supper. There was no ignoring it; the supper hour was writ in stone. Indeed, from one end of the week to the other there was a predictable quality to family meals in the Bronx.

Sunday was the high point, a day which began with fasting before Mass and Communion. Actually, under the old dispensation, the fast began at midnight. Whatever you were up to the night before, whatever tasty snack was in your hand, you partied with one eye on the clock. At midnight the dance went on, but neither food nor drink would pass those Catholic lips. There was a certain pleasurable pang in all this self-denial that no doubt went beyond the religious impulse. It set us apart as people who lived up to high standards; it gave us a sense of rigor, of fine aristocratic purity and reserve. But after Mass we descended in hordes on the neighborhood deli and made off with packages of baked ham, roast beef, seeded rolls, and black pudding kept by the Dutch deli man for Irish customers.

After lunch we sat around reading the funnies, took sedate walks in our Sunday dresses, watched the boats on the river, and otherwise killed time before settling down with aunts and uncles and cousins to a splendid roast with all the trimmings. Through the week thereafter, the main chance for supper was meat loaf or hamburger or stew. The leftovers, pasted with mayonnaise and slapped between two pieces of Wonder bread, reemerged as school lunch. On Thursdays when pickings were slim, Agnes and I resorted to Velveeta cheese or onion sandwiches dosed with salt. Mother might bake a huge soda bread dotted with raisins and caraway seeds; hot from the oven, topped with butter, it was delicious. Friday, naturally, was fish, frozen and disagreeable, a penitential meal. By Saturday—after Father's paycheck was cashed—we were on the upswing again.

For all my passionate interest in food, I never learned much about cooking in the Bronx. For a time at eleven or twelve, with a girlfriend I devoted Saturday afternoons to baking brownies and oatmeal cookies. We were making objects out of plaster of Paris at the same time; both homemade products had much the same consistency. When my own children were small, I mastered the art of cupcake making—both chocolate and vanilla—so the poor things would not be disgraced before their peers. But cooking as an art form or even as a pleasurable and comforting activity had little appeal until much later in life. A good daughter, slicing up the beans or washing up the dishes, I nonetheless resisted the domestic norm. The last thing in the world I wanted to be was a housewife. In high school my electives were math and science; I wouldn't be caught dead in home economics.

Agnes and I shared a room in the University Avenue apartment, which was shabby but comfortable, furnished with more or less the same objects for the sixteen years I lived there. We rearranged things or touched them up with paint; very little was ever discarded. Our four rooms with a view included a large bath and kitchen, and weirdly long halls stretching from the living room to our parents' bedroom and from our room to the front door. At six and seven, before I had become a full-fledged terror in the streets, I was often terrified at night by sulfurous dreams in which I was pursued by hairy beasts and fanged serpents (phallic implications, certainly). Half paralyzed with fear, I would creep down the long, long hallway to Mom and Dad and safety. Poor Agnes was left behind to be devoured.

When I was younger still, I dreamed of the fish that used to be displayed in large tanks at our fish store, the floor of which was heavily strewn with sawdust. There was a variety of fish, swarms of them, bulking at the bottom, level with my eyes. I watched while they were hauled out, gasping, onto large wooden chopping blocks, their bellies ripped open, the entrails spilling out. Blood streaked the aprons of the fish men, though the blocks were wiped immediately clean. Large, dark, cold fish, white bellied, they seemed to be waiting for the knife, numb in the water of the tank, not swimming around gaily like the angel fish or the striped guppies that were pets. At night I dreamed of them. They were flat, toothless, but swam over me in immense numbers, insistent, overpowering, even monotonous in their bulk and inevitability. Evicted from the warm comfort of my parents' bed, alone in the dark living room, east of the Grand Concourse, I was terrified. I dreamed of them for years.

Although I was my sister's staunch defender in public, Agnes and I did plenty of squabbling in the privacy of our room on University Avenue. This squabbling became more heated when we were older and I could no longer regard her as "the baby," a more or less benign figure, to be treated with affection and never taken seriously as a rival. From infancy she grew into a solemn little tot, shy but hospitable, inviting neighbors in for tea when Mother was looking the other way. At nine or ten, however, Agnes had pronounced views and pronounced preferences. Whereas I wavered and brooded over a course of action, she would not budge once she had taken a position. In time she even grew to be taller than I was, a serious affront to which I could only respond with mockery, a favorite ploy on both sides: "Oh, Agnes's feet are as green as the grass, and the boys all stare when they see her pass/one foot here on the curbstone fine; the other way down on the trolley line."

At one point our differences took the palpable form of painting our room two different colors. The dividing line was drawn through the dead center. The pink side—mine—was embellished with ruffled bedspread and curtains, pleasurably starched and ironed year after year out of fitful longings to be fragilely feminine. On the blue side was Agnes's neatly tailored bed, the radio, the bookstand, and the bleeding heart of Jesus— three square feet of it. For twenty years Agnes had to look up at that heart bleeding down over her drop by drop, the mournful face of Jesus inclined toward her as she slept . . . nervously. Would the whole thing collapse on top of her in the night? She got the holy water and the blessed palm, too. My side was secular.

Agnes's growing height had one distinct advantage: It got us into movies after five o'clock. During the day I advanced on the ticket office looking much younger than my thirteen or fourteen years (an attribute that disappeared with time, although it could have been even more useful later on). While Agnes lurked around the corner, I purchased two half-price tickets. In the evening we reversed the process, becoming adults so they would let us in. I never understood how the good old Ogden Avenue Theatre stayed in business with such crooks as ourselves as patrons.

A child's admission fee for a Saturday matinee was twelve cents; it was fifty cents for "adults" in the evening. The first one hundred kids to arrive for the matinee received a bonus—a comic book or a package of gum. The show went on for four hours, offering a double feature, eight cartoons, and one or two cliff-hangers, which we followed episode by episode from Saturday to Saturday, as well as the "News of the World." When that MGM lion roared, we were transported to paradise. Of course for the same fifty cents, we could go literally to a paradise created by Loew's Theatres and luxuriate in thick red velour, plushly upholstered seats, balconies hung with crystal chandeliers and fitted out with sumptuous baroque flourishes. Loew's Paradise on the Grand Concourse near

Fordham Road had as well softly rotating lights, starry in design, and goldfish swimming in a marble bowl. In the 1950s it was a great place to go with a date and then to Krums afterwards for an orgy of ice cream.

Agnes and I usually went to the movies together, although we didn't always go to the *same* movie. From ages ten to fourteen we had different tastes. I liked adventure, mystery, tales of bloodshed and horror, pythons dropping out of trees onto unwary travelers, and whole families swallowed up by earthquakes, their hands waving above the cracks. For a while Agnes suffered in silence, her eyes riveted on the red exit sign. Then she rebelled and went off to a musical comedy. Whoever left the movie first waited for the other at the bus stop. She usually rode. I usually walked, thriftily saving five cents, but we always arrived home together. Otherwise we'd never get out again.

How we loved those old movies! Like the radio programs of the 1940s—*The Lone Ranger, The Green Hornet, Superman, Inner Sanctum*—they fed our hunger for color and adventure, showed us people who led daring and romantic or, at least, different lives: Dana Andrews in his lone fighter over the Pacific, Fred Astaire and Ginger Rogers dancing on a penthouse roof overlooking Manhattan. At the movies we saw Paris with Gene Kelly and the West with Gene Autry, splendid even in black and white. Driving through Monument Valley, Utah, in the 1980s was like driving through an old MGM movie set. I kept expecting a "band of Indians" to come racing along the mesa. The movies shaped our expectations, showed us an America that was beautiful and glamorous. We weren't aware that it was racist or sexist. We wanted to be cowboys, too.

We all loved Westerns. Mother wanted to see the horses and the green fields; Dad wanted the showdown at the O.K. Corral. The virtues these movies presented were familiar ones. The hero always had the best horse, there was plenty of singing, and the bad guys were vanquished at the end. Actually Dad never had much time for movies, but there was usually a paperback Western in his back pocket when he went off to work. He traded back and forth with his cronies on the subway, hoarding favorites like Louis L'Amour and Zane Grey. There they were twenty feet underground, locked in a change booth, and dreaming of the Wild West. I later suspected that in their own way, led by the redoubtable Michael Quill, they were reliving and refighting the old Irish wars, bringing them to much more satisfactory conclusions.

On holidays and summer evenings entertainment was closer to home. It was then that our building superintendent, Tom Reilly, played the accordion loudly and plaintively while the neighbors gathered for a dance. The shouts and singing, the pounding rhythms of their feet, shook the windows of the fourth floor. Red-eyed, our heads muffled in our pillows, Agnes and I reeled along with them through "The Walls of Limerick," "The Siege of Ennis," "The Stack of Barley." On and on through the night. There were limits to our enthusiasm for the old country.

On normal days Mr. Reilly was a mild, neat little man with a wiry mustache, who worked long, poorly paid hours for some New York City department, just like everyone else's father. His wife was a stout, disheveled woman who produced nine children, the smaller ones as tattered and grimy as herself. She had a hard life, no doubt of it, raising a family in a cramped basement apartment, hauling up the dumbwaiter and hauling out the trash. Each week she mopped the floors of the entire building from top to bottom with little perceptible change in its appearance.

Moving slowly and heavily she swung her greying curls along with the mop—the *cailleach** herself, wrathful and sour. In all that din of conversation, she rarely spoke and looked much the same winter and summer shuffling along under an old shawl on slippered feet. Her younger children, in the cruel way of the street, were taunted and abused. They were the shanty Irish, the steerage crew, kept below decks when everyone else had become clean and respectable.

AN IRISH FATHER

In earliest memory Father pulls my sled through a deepening field of snow. In the distance is an immense fir tree. There is no one else in the park, no cars moving along the Concourse. The distant tree is suddenly, unexpectedly, ablaze with light; the brightly colored balls, red and gold, sway in the light wind. Darkness is falling with the soft hiss of snow, the crackle of ice under the sharp runners. We glide in a steady arc toward the glowing tree.

* Proverbial Irish hag, a force of nature.

There was never another tree quite like that, though Father carried one home for us every Christmas and ceremoniously set it up in the living room.

He was a sturdy, purposeful man with blue eyes, black curly hair, and a provoking smile. When he was about to tell us a terrible joke, the corners of his mouth would twitch, and we knew we were in for it. "Success to temperance," he would blithely intone, swallowing a glass of whiskey. There was a ritual quality to these jokes which we came to expect along with regular meals and a certain testiness about the electric bill. He liked to keep busy indoors as well as out. Not your typical Irishman, he peeled potatoes and scoured pots and pans as readily as he chopped wood or planted a vegetable garden. He seldom relaxed even with a book—he was a history buff—or newspaper and pipe in hand. He rattled the pages, thumped at the headlines, hunted through his pockets for matches or tobacco. The sheer vigor of his disposition, the peculiar brisk motion of his body, suggested optimism, a certainty that things could be done. It took us many years to discover the hidden vein of fatalism, which he perhaps unconsciously resisted, but which revealed itself treacherously under great stress.

Daniel Waters was born on a "fair-sized" farm in 1904 in Sligo on the west coast of Ireland. Yeats's country, between the sea and the great heathery hump of Ben Bulben. He used to climb to the summit as a boy to plant the Irish tricolor, which was predictably shot down by the local police and as predictably replaced by aspiring young Republicans.

When he was eight years old he lost his father, a progressive farmer whose family had prospered while he was alive but whose widow was left with little money and seven young children to raise. My father was the third child and the second son; there were five sisters. Relations stepped in, an uncle in particular, who put the boys, "humpty-backed rogues," to work in the fields while the girls looked after the chickens and geese. Their mother was explicit enough: Unless everyone helped, they'd all be sent off to the poorhouse. The two oldest eventually went to work for the Gore-Booths at Lissadell, as members of the family had for generations.

Father liked to tell us the legends of the "Big House" and about the cruelty of an earlier landlord, Sir Robert, the grandfather of Josslyn Gore-Booth and of Eva and Constance, who as young women were admired by Yeats ("Two girls in silk kimonos, both/Beautiful, one a gazelle"). Among the terrible events in local memory was the 1840s eviction of tenants who were shipped out for America aboard the Pomonore. ("Bad luck to you, Sir Robert and likewise Lady Gore,/who banished those poor people aboard the Pomonore.") The timbers were rotten, and the ship foundered within sight of land, drowning all the tenants on board. The crew manned the lifeboats and escaped, or so the story goes. There was a curse on the Gore-Booth family after that.

As a boy Father found Lissadell a thriving, hospitable place with orchards and gardens—there were twenty acres of poppies—where the children of tenants were welcomed and treated to games and gifts of food. During World War I, Josslyn Gore-Booth started an ammunition factory, which provided work for the local people. Any man who served with the British army was promised his job back, wounded or not, "and he kept his word." During the Troubles Gore-Booth remained neutral. When he was taken hostage by the Irish Republican Army, Father was one of the men who guarded him; "a cold man" but "a courageous one" who expected to be shot at any moment in reprisal. No matter what was done "to provoke him," he never called in the police. That's probably why Lissadell escaped burning, unlike many of the houses belonging to the landlords.

Lissadell had a strong hold on my father's imagination. Though he was skeptical and humorous by nature, it lingered in his memory as the place of romance and became for me an image that opened up the many-sidedness of history and the need to situate myself in relation to the past. I suppose that house was, paradoxically, a point of origin for our family, breeding expectations of grace and permanence, harboring as well the canker of disappointment.

When I visited Lissadell in 1970, the fields of poppies and the orchards were in ruins. The building, a bare grey limestone, was much smaller than I had imagined. Two elderly residents, desperate for a little income, had opened the lower floor to the public. One could see that many of the rooms must have been lovely once, particularly the music gallery with its high ceiling and tall windows looking out over the lawn. But the flowered chintz covering the furniture was badly worn, and the woman, who announced herself as the niece of Constance Markiewicz, the family rebel and one of the leaders of the 1916 rising, was trying in an embarrassed way to sell watercolors. She told one or two jokes in the English manner, standing on the staircase in the company of various stuffed birds. Her brother, white-haired but still handsome, offered pleasantries about Frank Sinatra.

Pulling out some old account books, the woman told us how the Gore-Booths had gone into debt to save their tenants during the famine. Still haunted by the ghosts of the Pomonore. Following along with the other tourists, I felt as though the poor woman were being forced to appear in her underwear. I kept quiet for fear of making matters worse. What could she say to me, the descendant of people who had worked for her family eleven hours a day and a half-day on Sunday; whose uncle, killed in the revolution, had been their chauffeur; whose father had held their grandfather prisoner?

Despite the harsh facts of his early life, Father's stories were usually full of gaiety and adventure. He was fond of telling us about his school years, mainly about tricks played on the way to school—such as children riding horses and donkeys belonging to neighbors until they were bucked off—and the perpetual skirmishing with the schoolmaster. A favorite joke was to bring in hazelnuts along with the daily offering of turf. In the midst of a fire the nuts would burst, shooting through the room to provide a glorious climax to the lesson. Punishment was brisk: a rod smartly applied to the upturned palms of the usual culprits. But the undercurrent of rebellion was never checked. If the master routed them all one day, he found mysterious holes in his bicycle tires the next. This was no Jesuit institution.

Judging from the family skills, lessons, when they could be gotten to in an ordinary Irish classroom, centered around poetry and math. At family parties, if they were not talking about death or politics, it was not unusual for someone, adopting a formal rhetorical stance, to offer lines from a poem. Father preferred to regale us with favorite and lengthy passages, usually by Walter Scott, as an incentive to housework. The more inappropriate the occasion, the better he liked to play out the lines in curious, lilting mockery. Thus, peeling a mound of potatoes, he would intone "The Lady of the Lake":

> The stag at eve had drunk his fill,
> Where danced the moon on Monan's rill,

And deep his midnight lair had made
In lone Glenartney's hazel shade. . . .

He also liked to recite certain prayers and humorous rhymes in English, Irish, and Latin. He actually knew little Irish because the old language was disparaged in Sligo at the turn of the century. People were afraid it would put a "curwhibble" or twist in the tongue, spoiling their English. He recalled being challenged during the revolution by a very nervous Irish-speaking sentry. On a scouting mission and out of uniform at the time, he avoided being shot by summoning a few scraps of the native tongue: *"Cen chaoi a bhfuil tú?"* (How are you?). His feeling for the old language nonetheless ran deep, linking him perhaps to the voices of his childhood. When he was dying in New York in 1983, he prayed in Irish.

When we were children he tested our ingenuity with mathematical "ticklers." "How many feet have forty sheep, a shepherd, and his dog?" He could blithely juggle two unknowns in his head to solve an algebra problem I couldn't puzzle out: "If the head and tail of a fish was twice as long as the body, and the body was half again the size of the tail . . ." He often worked twelve—or sixteen-hour shifts, coming home late at night and polishing off a homework problem left along with a sandwich on the kitchen table. He would shake his head in pity at me the next morning at breakfast.

There was always a measure of dissent between our parents on the subject of the old country. Father liked to give us all the down-to-earth details. "Disgusting!" Mother would call them, yanking at the lace curtains. But Father would go right on talking about the *bonhams* or young pigs snuggled in by the fireplace, or describing with relish some awful practical joke, like the time some friends found a neighbor in a drunken stupor with his donkey and cart in the middle of the road. With consummate patience they dismantled the cart and then reassembled the whole rig, the beast included, inside the man's house. As a parting gesture they covered the windows with sod, so the poor man woke up thinking he was in Hell. "He was sober a long time after that one."

Father told us stories over and over again because we loved to hear them, though no doubt there was a level of instruction here, too, a concern with history, with values celebrated in local lore and passed down to us, the Irish dimension to our education. Always fond of jokes, he recalled the wild humor loosed at Halloween or *Samhain* and at wakes—a great source of pipe tobacco when he was a boy. He told stories about the revolution and the cruelty of the Black and Tans; stories about his brother, Michael, who died in the war; stories about animals and about local characters.

He remembered shipwrecks off the western coast of Ireland during World War I. Timber and other useful articles would float in with the tide. Once a big bay stallion swam to shore still tethered to the remains of his heavy wooden stall. "Whoever got their mark on this stuff before it touched dry land got to keep it, that is, if the police did not get there first, and they could not be everywhere."

There were other sea stories, too, because some of the family had lived on Inishmurray Island, some nine miles off the coast of Sligo. A place of sudden, violent storms, where a boat had to be maneuvered skillfully to avoid hitting the rocks where you went ashore at Clashymore Harbor. The island has a long, eventful history recorded in the annals as early as the seventh century.

There is an ancient *cashel* on the island which may be pre-Christian in origin. This stone enclosure contains several buildings of beehive construction; there are chapels and a schoolhouse. Inishmurray was once a pilgrimage site; the stone stations and large "praying stones," some with curious holes in them, are still visible around the perimeter of the island. There are local accounts of miracles and Viking raids; certain marks near the main chapel are reputed to be the bloodstains of scholars killed by raiders in 802. In the nineteenth century, however, it was an ideal spot for poteen makers, who lived comfortably in sturdy houses apart from the war and famine that periodically swept the mainland. Along with the "praying stones" on the island were still to be found altars on which "cursing stones" had been placed. According to the story, these were used against the odd tariff man who attempted to levy a tax on the islanders. Turning the stones counterclockwise and pronouncing the appropriate curses made it difficult for him to reach shore alive.

In Sligo one summer I inquired about a boat to Inishmurray. I was welcomed cordially, though there was no hope because the usual storm was brewing. Members of the Waters family, I was reminded, had been "kings" of Inishmurray, a peculiar fact to mull upon, given that the island is one mile long and about one-half mile wide. The people must have had a powerful sense of territoriality. It turned out that for nearly one hundred years a man named Waters had alternated with a man named Heraughty (an archeological report refers to "rival dynasties") as the leader—a combination doctor, schoolmaster, carpenter, lawyer, and man of all trades. When my father visited there as a boy, a great-uncle named Waters was still at the helm, but the last of the tribe were taken off the island during the 1940s. The hardship finally proved too extreme.

These stories made a deep impression on us as children, linking us firmly to the old country, though our parents never went back in later years when they could afford to do so. We were early made aware of the perilousness of that old life. Gaiety would shift suddenly into sadness. Ireland was never simply the land of shamrocks and leprechauns or a memory celebrated on St. Patrick's Day. Too many had died, too many were disappointed. The hard fight for independence, the bitter aftermath of civil war, did not bring prosperity. Emigration went on. The old family home under Ben Bulben collapsed in ruin.

Michael, my father's older brother, died at seventeen from wounds received in a futile attack on a military garrison in 1920. A bomb he was carrying exploded in his hands. When he died a few days later, he was buried secretly in an unmarked grave—his name still on a list of wanted men—because the family feared reprisals. Their house might be burned like so many others in the village of Cloonelly; someone else might be killed. My father's name was on the same list. But we only learned this gradually, perhaps because the memory was so painful, perhaps because the facts themselves were ambiguous. At first we heard that Michael had died from a fall, and then that he had died of a weak heart, which is what they told the militia hunting for him after the attack.

Visiting Sligo for the first time twenty-five years ago, I felt compelled to hunt for the grave of this lost uncle. Two of his sisters were with me, pacing back and forth, trying to settle on the exact spot where he had been interred at night without a ritual of any kind. They thought they knew where it was, so we stood there together in remembrance, one of them intoning the customary words of acceptance: "Ah well, it was the will of God." In pre-Christian times his death would have been ascribed to fate or, as in that most poignant of early tales, *The Destruction of Da Derga's Hostel,* to the hero Conaire's violation of certain codes of justice. Michael had been carrying a bomb. Perhaps that is why Father invariably offered a prayer, "The Lord have mercy on him," which came to sound like part of his name: "Michael, the Lordtamercyonim." No one else, out of the long litany of "dear departed," was remembered in this fashion.

So there it is. The prototypical family story of two brothers, close in age. One was level-headed, "lucky," a survivor in hard times; the other, impetuous, drawn to danger, willing it, imprinting a scar that never healed.

There was a sister, too, whose story was eclipsed by the story of Michael, to whom Father was deeply attached and for whom he always grieved. That was Ann. The exact time is uncertain. She was recovering from pneumonia when a storm came up while the hay was being gathered in. Because at fifteen she was the oldest and strongest child at home, she went out to help in the fields, suffered a relapse, and died. No doctor would come because of the curfew. I know little else about her except that she could not be persuaded to stay inside. She had the family stubbornness all right. I think of her now as one of those anonymous women who stand in the gap just behind the front lines. About whom no songs are sung, though the war killed her just as surely as it killed her brother.

Daniel, my father, also fought in the Anglo-Irish War and was with the Free State artillery unit that shelled the Four Courts at the start of the civil war in 1922. Thereafter he served as a medical corpsman, more and more troubled by the mounting casualties, the hatred, and the waste of life. He went out under fire, poorly trained and poorly equipped to retrieve the dead and wounded, crossing through IRA territory where other ambulances had been burned and the corpsmen lined up and shot. He served in the cavalry, nursed IRA prisoners on hunger strike, was promoted to sergeant major, and then landed in jail, having fired a shot that accidentally pierced the cap of a Brigadier McHugh. As he told it, this was a war that veered sharply in direction and intensity. There were pleasant lulls when the men took Irish dancing lessons in Castlebar, where—he liked to speculate—he might have met Mother. But his best friend was killed by a sniper as they walked together through that same town. It was guerrilla warfare marked by ambush, bloody reprisals, and much dirty detail work. From one of these ambushes he once rescued his old schoolmaster, who had lost an arm but was still able to joke: "If you only knew it was me, Danny, you'd have taken much longer to get through."

After all this Father never imbued us with any hatred of the English but imparted a sense of his own gaiety and courage as a young man. At sixteen, seventeen, and eighteen, he was drawn to the edge of existence and felt its strangeness, its inexplicability, its cruelty. A deeply religious man, he never resorted to pieties, but he believed that "something good comes from every experience." I realize now that telling those stories, imprinting them on our minds as children, was one way of recuperating what was lost.

When he wasn't talking, Father appeared unassuming, even nondescript in well-worn blue or brown gabardine. In later years, earning a decent salary, he scarcely changed; he never developed the acquisitiveness of the middle class. Apart from books and a few pieces of clothing, his belongings, including the memoir he left to us, could be fitted into one bureau drawer. But his modest manner concealed a fierce, fundamental pride. Though he was well read and politically astute, he would listen deferentially to men in suits who had a better formal education. He was respectful toward nuns and priests. We knew, however, that beyond a certain point, moral or political, he would not budge. Put a gun to his head—as two New York thugs once did—and he would not capitulate. Given enough pressure, unjust or wrongheaded, and the hot temper at the core of the man boiled to the surface. He hit back.

After his death, I discovered that he had taken part in the army mutiny of 1924. After nearly five years of fighting to establish an Irish government, he took up arms against it. What were his motives? Outrage? Disillusionment? Loyalty to officers he served with? It appears that with an end to the civil war, many of the old social barriers were re-erected. Men who had fought well were cashiered, their places taken by the better educated and those with family and political connections. Perhaps that was it. The fact remains that when his ambulance was used secretly by the rebels to ferry rifles and machine guns, he agreed to join them. After the mutiny collapsed, he was broken to the ranks and sent to the Curragh for "retraining." He received an honorable discharge—all the grievances to some extent recognized—but he was a marked man after that. In a sense I owe my existence to that mutiny. When the military hierarchy offered to review his case in Dublin, he turned them down. In 1927 he took the boat to America and never went back.

Landing in New York on the eve of the Depression, he found at first only poorly paid, backbreaking construction jobs, where the bosses re-garded all Irishmen as drunken, irresponsible, fit only for the dirtiest kind of work. The barriers were still there. But many less able individuals got through those barriers and made for themselves more satisfying material lives. At some point my father seems to have made peace with the world in which he found himself. No doubt marriage had something to do with this. Having grown up in poverty and come of age in the middle of a rev-olution, he badly needed security. It was an essential quality in the home he made for us. There was an emotional bedrock that we could depend on.

He retained, and no doubt passed on to us, a lively skepticism and a resistance to notions of class: "If you have to go in your two bare feet, you're as good as the next fellow." He had a way of closing doors with great finality. But he was seldom bitter. He liked his cronies in the New York subway where, like so many Irishmen, he eventually found work; there was plenty of time for talk in the lull between morning and evening rush hours. He lived for his family, for the books and music he enjoyed, and the country house he eventually built. Accepting his modest portion in life, he was boundlessly optimistic for us. We were American-born, and we would be educated. A feminist in his own way, it was fine with him that we were girls.

MAYO WOMAN

Mother remains loyal to the IRA, harboring at eighty very hostile designs on the person of Maggie Thatcher. There is no use speaking to her of moderation or the casualties of civil war: "A daring fellow is the jewel of the world." Her memory of the boys on the run is unfailingly romantic, unfailingly green. In arguments with Father she held up the rebel stan-dard of Michael, his dead brother, "a real patriot," not "a compromiser." You could tell she would have married Michael at the drop of a hat if she had only met him in time.

The judgments of history are meaningless to her as are all the inter-vening years. It is still the 1920s in Ireland. When I offer her a few sober details about the antitreaty forces or the violence in Belfast, she renders me speechless with scorn: "You read that in a book." She corrects and amends my account of Dublin, visited regularly during the last twenty years, to bring it in line with her own recollections of some fifty years before. "It was dangerous to go into Phoenix Park." She had never seen "so many poor people as they had in Dublin." She didn't like Dublin "a-tall."

It is her own personal history that matters, and now she is reconstructing that. I can't tell any longer which is fact and which is fiction. New details keep coming to light in new versions of the old stories. Part of this is loss of memory, wishful thinking, a new view of herself, a new relationship to us, her daughters: "We all had to go out to work." Part of it is cunning. She is still intent on pummeling her own values into us. She prays obsessively, laying siege to God, winning Him over to her side, making Him arrange things the way she wants them. A case in point: I've been ill. I've had extensive surgery, but now I'm going to be just fine. She's seeing to it. In convents and churches throughout New York City and points west a chorus of prayers goes up daily on my behalf.

When we were all much younger, I was convinced Mother could read my mind. There were no lies in our household. Under her penetrating eye, we didn't get away with much. One New Year's Eve, given the impossible curfew of midnight, we turned the clock back one hour. A pretty dopey plan that reveals how little hope we had of success. Naturally, we were locked out and had to plead to get in. Not only could she quickly divine when we were up to no good, she could sense it beforehand.

Mother dreams. Even in our family, all with one foot on some extraterrestrial plane, she's in a class by herself. Her conversation is hinged with omens and portents and dire predictions connected with the weather. To dream of a horse or a field of flowers is lucky. So, of course, is the color green. My phone will ring emphatically at eight in the morning. "Is everything all right???" She has seen trouble: wasted fields, storms, a coiled snake. If I don't answer, she assumes I'm dead on the floor just out of reach of her voice. She has an instinct for disaster. There's been an explosion on the Upper West Side. Have I felt it? Has it damaged our apartment or, perhaps, my eardrums? Once she dreamed she saw me running down the street dressed only in my Maidenform bra. (This was truer than she realized at the time.) Now when she can't make up her mind, or she is afraid to fly to California to visit Agnes and her family, Father appears in her dreams. He is parking the car and will be around to the door directly. He tells her to stop worrying.

She has earnest conversations with Brian Patrick, forging new bonds of kinship and sympathy. My rebel son is a lad to her taste. When did this happen? Brian set out at the age of sixteen, thumbing his way across America, calling us intermittently late at night to let us know he was just fine and had no intention of coming back for a few more years. "Do you like being a terror?" she asks. He does. So does she. "No use being too nice. People take you for granted." Solid grandmotherly advice.

The proverbial Irish shape changer, she has shifted her allegiances, to say nothing of her character and disposition over and over with the years. We were always certain about Father, knew what he would tolerate, knew what he believed in. He was rock bottom dependable. Even when we left the Church and went off with the wrong men, we knew he would forgive us eventually. With Mother we were less certain. She was as unpredictable as spring weather, punishing and kindly by turns, and we could never tell which turn or whose turn it would be.

She is one of the most willful people I have ever known. A born combatant, touchy, quick to take offense, manipulative, possessive. In her heyday, so full of energy, so shrewd and ready with advice, she could have run Amtrak and made a profit. She often prodded us with stories of the hard life in Mayo, and used aphorisms delivered with ironic effect: "Birds in their little nests agree" (when Agnes and I were strangling one another); "a stitch in time saves nine" (when a hem completely unraveled). She was also fond of hortatory verse: "Standing at the foot, girls, gazing at the sky/How can you get up, girls, if you never try!" Thus she encouraged amity, foresight, and determination. And if that failed, she took out the mop and put us to work.

She was a doting, benevolent mother in my early years—hospitable, mild-mannered, and lovely in her velvet cloche hats and well-tailored dresses. She taught us to look at sunsets, stars, lake water. While Father had eyes only for the tomatoes he was coaxing to grow in our backyard, Mother planted roses, sweet peas, pansies, nasturtiums, and embroidered a trail of flowers across the sweaters she used to knit. When she was pregnant, she spent afternoons listening to music and went out of her way—

being cooped up in a city—to find paintings of beautiful landscapes, expecting this would have a salutary effect on her unborn child. Hers was an aesthetic eye.

In my teens she was an angry, moody woman, who suffered from migraine headaches and made us dread coming home from school, particularly on days when she had been out working. Her voice would reproach us: We were guilty of something, but what had we done? What was wrong? She would shake her head or begin to weep hysterically: "You wouldn't understand." Which made us suspect Father had done something terrible. In truth, what we could never understand was the humiliation she felt, an Irishwoman forced to sell bedspreads in Macy's because her husband couldn't support the family. Taunted by other women: "Haven't you a husband?" (did she imagine this?), Mother retreated inside a bubble of narcissism, alone and helpless, disgusted with all of us. A perpetually injured party, she was troubled by the first signs of an enlarging fear and finally a hatred of the outside world and of anyone and anything that was different, foreign. "Why are they all coming in here?"

From this position she duly emerged a sunny, benevolent grandmother with a liking for California and fast cars (unless I'm driving). She has been through several cycles since then.

Nothing has value to her unless she can talk about it. She regards me as supremely naïve, an innocent, "always with your nose in a book," and consequently little grasp of reality: "You don't know what's going on." Reality is what people say. What they do is mainly a preliminary to what can be said about it. She has little sense of our professional lives, although she's pleased we have them. It's the family life that's important. And within that charmed circle she is the grande dame.

For much of my life I have struggled against her. I fear her fears.

In front of me now is a passport photo dated February 3, 1925. She was nineteen. The figure is badly dressed, the heavy dark blond hair knotted clumsily at the back of the head. The face, turned to one side, is homely and uncertain. Stamped on the passport is the name, Bridget Ruane. Bridget is her mother's name, but a name also associated with ignorant, comical Irish maids. In the photo attached to her citizenship papers, she faces the camera decisively. Her dress is fringed in lace; her hair curls lightly along newly prominent cheekbones, but there is an unmistakable sadness in her countenance. Three years later, on the first baptismal certificate, her name appears as Agnes—a new personality in keeping with her new status in America. The name will be passed on to her younger daughter, in hope, no doubt, of releasing her, too.

In photos from middle age she seems someone else altogether: angry, overweight, dowdy; her hair tightly permed, her eyes receded as though she could no longer see clearly or had little interest in what was out there. Standing in front of my old house in Seaview, Long Island, she appears utterly indifferent to the five-year-old granddaughter beside her, rolling her eyes. She wears a fussy small hat weighted with flowers, a mink stole clutched over her abdomen, sturdy shoes, a short plain skirt. None of it suits her.

Mother was born in Mayo in 1906 on a small farm whose fields still carried Gaelic names, Tor an Chor, Cnoc an Phortaigh, and the Cúlán. Where it was remembered that famine victims had been buried. She was the third of eight children; six daughters and one son survived, a painfully significant ratio in rural Ireland. The Ruane family was poor like most of their neighbors in that beautiful, haunted western world that fired the imagination of John Synge. Their lot was harder than most because the father, a thin, spare man with a ginger mustache and a liking for politics, was unsuited to farming. When times were especially hard, he went to England to find work, leaving the family uncertain of his whereabouts. One year he collapsed with fever and almost died, was in fact pronounced dead and placed in a coffin, but he climbed out of the coffin and returned home, "though his health was uncertain after that."

Mother's memories of her early years are bitter, though she insists that there were good times, too. gathering in the hay, trips to the nearby town of Castlebar, dancing with the boys "on the run." There was heavy fighting in their part of the country during the Anglo-Irish War that started in 1919 and the civil war that followed in 1922. Trains were blown up, police barracks were attacked, and there were reprisals. From the beginning her sympathies were staunchly Republican. Her brother was too young to take part in the Troubles, but cousins fought the British and then took the Republican side in the civil war. They were jailed and tortured, their teeth smashed, their bones broken.

During those turbulent years the calm center of life was her own mother, whom she likes to remember passing her good dress out the window so she could slip off to a dance despite the father's injunctions. This was an uncharacteristic gesture of resistance in one revered as the archetypal Good Mother, patient, enduring, tending the fire in the hearth, the candle in the window. Whom none of us has managed to emulate. Was she really like that? In photos my grandmother is stern, her features marked by physical pain, her dark hair and eyes revealing the Spanish blood intermingled with that of the Ó Súilleabháins. In one photo she appears with my Aunt Frances, only seven or eight then with her beautiful thick hair closely cropped about her head. Neither looks at the other and both are unsmiling. In another she sits heavily in a chair, the folds of a dark coat gathered around her; in the background roses are growing all along the side of the house.

The poet Eavan Boland has described women as living "outside history," that is, outside the political, social, patriarchal nexus of power. Her immediate reference is Ireland, where history is all too palpable and oppressive. It is curious to see something of the same process at work in family chronicles, where women are fitted into a hallowed niche of memory, revered but static figures, inspiring little curiosity or reflection.

There is no photo of my grandfather, of whom Mother rarely speaks. Apparently he was a harsh, occasionally violent man. The archetypal Irish father who forced his daughters, six of whom were born before the one son, to work in the fields when they should have been in school. He made them feel they had done him a grave injustice by being born female. Seventy years later Mother still burns with the humiliation of falling behind her class and of running away to avoid being slapped. Her mother taught her to read and write.

By the time she was twelve she had learned to stand her ground against her father, and she refused to budge when she was threatened in school, unlike Frances, who was terrified of the teachers. When Frances finally left school she smashed all the inkwells one by one in the creek where she had been sent to wash them. When war broke out—a story Mother likes to tell—and soldiers ransacked their house looking for rifles, she stopped them from overturning the cradle which held Eileen, the youngest child. She likes to remind Eileen of that. In the long run the father came to respect her, and he was apparently proud of her good looks. When she was fifteen he had a lovely green tweed suit made for her in Castlebar, planning a match with an older man with a good farm. She had nothing but contempt for this plan and did not forgive her father even as he grew milder and steadier with age.

The younger sisters provide a different perspective, remembering him as worn out by illness and hard work. A man who mourned his wife and, dying of cancer in middle age, he did not survive her for long. Eileen speaks of him with affection as a well-read, argumentative sort of man, who carried her out to the fields to keep him company while he worked. Surrounded by Republicans, he was militant against the nationalist movement. War meant havoc in rural areas, crops destroyed, cattle and horses run off; they were having a hard enough time surviving as it was. His resistance was rooted in history. An ancestor had landed with Humboldt's forces at Kinsale in 1798, had seen the Irish overpowered and slaughtered. He was a man of little optimism.

Grandfather Ruane remains a mystery, the short narrative of his life punctuated by ellipses, by the sudden repression of memory: "No need to speak ill of the dead." Among all the stories that are told and retold, there comes a point beyond which Mother will not go, things she will not tell us, even now. Of course it has occurred to me that there is nothing unusual hidden at all. She has a taste for drama, for turning on her heel with a gesture: "Never mind." But I'm not sure. I grew up with the impression of a dark secret in the family, something cruel and hidden, a touch of the Faulknerian souring those green fields. Pieces still churn to the surface: Grandfather Ruane was committed to a mental institution by his two oldest daughters—out of desperation? fury?—and quickly released as "sane." When British soldiers ransacked the house, looking for weapons, there were none because Mother had already given their rifle to the IRA. Was this patriotism, or fear that their father might shoot them all in a rage?

Eileen, in whom he used to confide, speaks of dowry money promised him—so it was an arranged marriage—but never given by the O'Sullivans, my grandmother's family. A terrible breach of the rural ethic and a great loss to a poor man. According to her story, he was badly beaten by his wife's people when he insisted on his rights. None of them was allowed in his house after that. This account is firmly denied by Mother, who liked the O'Sullivans; they had helped her and Margaret, the two oldest, to emigrate to America.

There is yet another strand to this gapped chronicle, about which all basically agree. It has to do with the loss of the first child, scalded to death when she upset a kettle of boiling water. She had been left in the care of her paternal grandfather, who failed to reach her in time. His son never forgave him. It was a story we listened to many times: that sudden, terrible death of the fair-haired, blue-eyed Ann; the unforgiving, grieving father. After we knew the original facts, many years later, the tale took an unexpected and sinister turn. It seems that not only the grandfather but Margaret, the next child born, and perhaps the mother were also blamed. Near the end of her life, Margaret told us how she was beaten by her father on the public road to Castlebar, ostensibly because she spoke out of turn, but in truth, because she was not, nor ever would be, the beautiful, sweet-tempered Ann.

Margaret often threatened to tell us more, or at least to commit the worst parts to a tape recording, which would then be placed in a vault for the next generation (the usual Irish inheritance). She wanted to spare us. "The things I could tell you," she would say, words which conjured up scenes of violence, incest, rape. She was a woman of vast imagination. Margaret probably had cancer, too. She had anticipated that for years, the fatal element in family history, as it were, imprinting itself in our genes. She refused all doctors: "I don't want them to touch me." And so she went on suffering, implacable, dying on her own terms without medication or advice, attended only by her husband, who struggled against waves of vomit and diarrhea to keep her clean. An older cousin of mine died in much the same way in shame and stubbornness, refusing to let any doctor touch her vagina until it was too late anyhow.

Stories about Ireland always had an agonizing strand running through them that was not entirely the result of poverty and the deprivation that went with it. The nuns who taught us tried hard to instill their simple, comforting moral categories. But their sense of a well-ordered universe was undermined by the corrosive currents of family history. At the very least there was a bitterness, an unresolved anger and disappointment embodied in my grandfather and passed on to his children, even as they left him for America.

After the death of their parents, the three youngest Ruanes, still in their teens, remained alone on the farm raising cattle. All Eileen seems to remember from that time were storms that were immensely destructive in the northwest near the sea. She was afraid that the thatched roof would be swept away and they would be left in the dark, exposed to the wind and rain. As soon as enough money could be saved by those who had emigrated, the two remaining girls followed them. The son abandoned the land, moved to the central part of Ireland, and took up residence in a town.

When I visited the old homestead in 1970, I found the stone walls still standing though the roof had long ago fallen in. It looked exactly like all the other small ruined cottages in the West of Ireland. I was impressed with the profound stillness of the place. Nothing moved. The interior of the house was spare and empty. The fireplace had collapsed. There were no clues to the former inhabitants, not a shred of furniture or a piece of crockery. All the particulars had vanished. Grass covered the little fields.

TRIBAL VOICES

When I was old enough to have a grasp of such matters, I kept a hopeful eye on Mother, eager for her to be pregnant and only waiting for the right moment to spring her surprise. I had no complaint against Agnes. But I felt gypped. Why weren't there more? A whole band to keep me company and hold the other brats at bay? What I got instead were immigrant aunts—not much help in a gang war, but nice enough in their way.

Mother's five sisters—Margaret, Patricia, Frances, Katherine, and Eileen—all eventually settled in New York City. We grew up fairly surrounded by lively, pretty, talkative aunts, each with a distinctive temperament and her own melancholy way of looking at the world. They were usually quick to find their way around the Irish-American network, acquiring jobs and apartments and a host of irrefutable opinions. But one fell headlong into our clutches. That was Frances, who was timid and trustful and hinted at experience with ghosts. She kept a notebook of poems, some of them her own, and would read to us sadly about "time's winged chariot hurrying near." We easily got the upper hand when she was left minding us, telling her frightful lies and terrorizing her with the kitchen knife so we could do exactly what we wanted. When we went out to the park together, we got her lost and then hid while she wandered around in confusion, eventually returning home in tears. But she never told on us or gave us (really me) the licking that was well deserved.

Indeed our aunts were all very indulgent. They listened to our stories, applauded our triumphs, sympathized with our woes. They were frequent and welcome visitors; our parents had few friends outside the family. Agnes and I were obviously important to them but, aside from the mishaps of the latest immigrant, the adults were indisputably in control. At holiday parties they dominated the conversation, which was incessant, discordant, humorous, and invariably accompanied by pots and pots of tea, a round of whiskey, plenty of butter and soda bread. They enjoyed peppering one another, following up the initial assault with another and yet another salvo perfectly and provokingly aimed. The family style was—and, indeed, still is—confrontational, disjunctive, given to mockery and rapid fire verbal explosion that knocks the whole party off balance. My aunts were seldom constrained by conventional notions of politeness. If you were looking awful, they would tell you so—graphically: "You're getting mud fat!" "Your eyes look like two burnt holes in a blanket!" Or, the horrified memory of a ten-year-old biting into a steak: "That'll put hair on your chest!"

This style is deeply ingrained in the second generation as well, producing in some of us a kind of social schizophrenia. Hearing smoothly harmonious conversation in which people listen reflectively to one another—the style of my husband, David's, family for instance—I feel like the stone in the midst of all. It is the inflected voice, the oscillating emotional rhythm that rouses me.

The novelist Mary Gordon has written about the conservative cast of her middle-class Irish family who invariably defer to the priest who is a relation. Rural West of Ireland families are different. Isolated from town and orthodox values, holding to their own opinions above all others, they are more likely to tolerate and, probably at some level, encourage the eccentric as adding spiciness to life. We have a fine, articulate priest in the family, too, but he has to take his lumps with the rest of us: "On water skis! That's the modern clergy for you. Next thing, he'll be skydiving." A college degree is no guarantee of escape either: "After all, you were born here." No one is spared the scalding mockery that seals our tribal love.

On holidays the family favored stories about funerals and grave sites.

Great-aunt Nora, the one who had long ago helped the older sisters to emigrate, had provided yet another haven in New York, a large, conveniently situated grave. They were fond of discussing how they would be interred there, in what order and in what position, and what their tombstone would be like. Would they have shamrocks or would they have trumpeting angels, the ethnic or the ecumenical motif? Aunt Patricia planned to be sitting up (for an easier exit, perhaps) both at her wake and in her penultimate resting place.

Patricia was my godmother, a pert, diminutive woman with black curly hair and fair unfreckled skin. She was a good painter and, with her bright uncivil eye, a better cartoonist. Her cards and letters invariably enclosed a witty drawing by way of commentary on our lives. One I particularly liked showed a line of uniformed schoolgirls, marching in perfect unison, the line flattening out from right to left, the bodies growing tiny but the feet monstrous in oxford shoes, the berets like flying saucers.

She took me to my first movie (about a horse), my first Broadway musical *(Oklahoma!)*, and my first show at Radio City on an Easter Sunday afternoon, featuring a leggy chorus of dancing vegetables. Why should that detail linger after fifty years? Probably because it was not what I expected. Aunt Patricia, with her little straw hat, navy blue purse and shoes, and her dependable box of cake, loved a surprise. She sometimes rang our front doorbell and hid, leaving a basket of candy or a stuffed animal, and when we touched it, she pounced. She was also given to the direct sexual remark that led a man to hastily check his fly, and poked newly married women to determine whether they were pregnant. "Something cooking in there?" And if not, "Why not? You've had time enough."

I liked her paintings of ships and flowers that hung above my bed and enjoyed going to the studio in Yorkville, where she worked, to meet her painter friends. But it seemed to me that she drew unholy numbers of neat little sheep grazing the hillsides of Mayo. For all her provocative remarks, her emotional life was mainly sealed off, perhaps even from herself. When she was in her twenties, Aunt Patricia entered a convent and fled the next day for reasons that were not explained. Probably she couldn't stand all those other nuns. Until she was burned out, she lived alone in a tiny apartment in Manhattan, devoutly attending daily Mass and reading poetry and philosophy, Thomas Merton, Teilhard de Chardin, William James. Always generous to us, she was indifferent to the usual objects that people acquire; she even gave her paintings away. I tried to imitate them, sketching sweet Jesus in pastel and painting ships and lighthouses in seas of blue and green watercolor. They were awful.

There was a decidedly matriarchal strain to family gatherings. Coming to this country, with little formal education, my aunts worked as waitresses and cashiers in Schraft's, but these jobs seemed to have little to do with their actual lives. Most of their considerable imaginative energy was focused on the family drama. While a holiday dinner brought all the players conveniently together, they seldom separated for long, communicating daily by phone and generating scene after scene of domestic crisis. They kept up a perpetual skirmish in which the sisters aligned themselves in coalitions against one another and as rapidly changed sides, shifted the balance of power, or withdrew in a huff. But never for long. A word was sufficient to set them off. They invariably anticipated the worst and delightedly filled in the most awful possibilities as the story grew in size and metamorphosed from one to the other. Very little was kept a secret for long, though everyone maintained a different version of the secret.

We knew all about the boyfriends who came courting to our apartment, willing and amiable, offering bribes to us kids, waiting to be approved. These unfortunates were discussed in comical-critical terms: This one had no decent shoes; another was miserably thin; another had rotten teeth. Men were regarded with a certain disdain, apart from, of course, our father and Uncle Stuart, two sturdy islands in this female sea. Our aunts were not keen on marriage, and so avoided it entirely or delayed as long as possible before taking the plunge. (Except for romantic Aunt Katherine, who eloped with the man she loved.) About the worst they would say of one another was, "Oh, she's playing up to the men. She's always trying to please the men."

Relations between women and men were a source of discomfort and occasionally of scandals that created problems three thousand miles away. The main one had to do with our mysterious Uncle Kevin, the only son, "born too late," after six daughters. We tried to imagine Kevin, the one who stayed behind and who, it turned out, lived with a woman to whom he was not married because she had a husband somewhere. There was no divorce in the Irish Free State or in the republic either. Kevin was not a respectable person. There was considerable misery over his predicament and over the question of how to regard his three daughters. Should they be recognized? Should they be taken into the family, that stronghold of virtue? The aunts were divided on these questions, which were discussed in heated but hushed tones that altered dramatically at the appearance of any of us children, so we always knew something was up and also assumed the worst. But in our family the claims of kinship ultimately won out over any other consideration, including the rules of the Church. No one objected to my divorce or to my second marriage with a much finer man. They were glad for me, perhaps excepting Mother, who maintained I should be happy enough with my books.

Years later when we finally met Kevin, a soft-spoken, heavyset man with lovely blue eyes, he told us how he and the woman he loved had been forced to move from town to town when people found them out. They were denounced publicly by the clergy, and her two young daughters were taken away by the husband who had originally abandoned them. Their own children were marked as illegitimate. Kevin grieved that he and Helena, a shy little woman with a rosy face and wispy yellow hair—no Hester Prynne—could not be buried together in a Catholic cemetery.

Beneath the laughter and the mercurial shifts in temper was always a gulf of sadness from which the great adventure in America did not distract my mother or her sisters for long. Moving in Irish circles, they found friends from "the other side," held on to ties that bound them to that bleak and beautiful homeland and that despairing father. They remained displaced persons, never fully at home on these expedient shores.

Despite all this it seems to me that the experience of the Waters family was more painful. When Dad was young, not only his father but three children died—there was a small girl, suffering from diphtheria, who actually choked to death in his arms. He was only eight at the time, and in the same year he lost his father. The Waters family are religious in a way I can scarcely comprehend. They never show fear. They never despair. They accepted these deaths and all the later cruel deaths of children and grandchildren as the will of God. I never heard them cry out. Unlike the Ruanes, who have a critical, doubting streak in them as well as a morbid sense of humor.

Mother never accepts calamity or even a minor setback with equanimity. Father was resigned in his last illness. Knowing he wouldn't survive the year, he ignored the doctors, went back in his dreams to Cloonelly, and began to pray in Gaelic. Mother battled on for both of them, though she tended to mislocate the crux of the tragedy. "Why me?" she railed, heaving the bedpan and driving another nurse to quit. "What have I ever done?"

Even now at eighty, she rejects the possibility that age might have something to do with her infirmities. Frail and tattered, her teeth missing, her hair a few miserable white clumps, she smiles with the charm of a twenty-year-old, accustomed to being admired and accustomed to getting her way, the one who danced on the boat "all the way to America" and disembarked with a proposal of marriage. Now, one minute raging against the doctors, she is suddenly all flattery and guile, her voice the voice of my childhood, able to charm the birds down from the trees, able to get around any doctor or priest or professor of English.

NUNS

The season of Christmas. Music, festivity, falling snow. A sense of rising expectation. Mother has fashioned a pair of cellophane wings and fitted them to my long nightgown. I am perhaps four years old. Aunt Katherine falls on her knees when I appear in the doorway, proclaiming me an angel of God. This is embarrassing, but the wings are very pretty and I enjoy floating around the apartment with them. Pausing before an open window, I am tempted to float out into the evening air. I consider this for several minutes, thinking I can probably manage it but not altogether certain.

Growing up in the Bronx, I was never altogether certain of boundaries between the old country and the new or between this world and the next. The deeply held Irish and Catholic convictions of our parents permeated our day-to-day lives. Our home had its icons, familial and spiritual; family myths blended with those fostered by religion. Our Gothic school was linked firmly to our Gothic church with all its lovely, time-honored ceremonies, the Mass in Latin, the soft chanting of the priest, the blaze of lilies at Easter. The sense of serene and living worship was communal as well as personal.

Our daily rhythms were punctuated by the beat of a celestial clock.

Each morning we awoke to the tolling bell of the Carmelite convent across the street. It tolled the hour of Mass, the hour for prayer, ringing out for the Angelus at six o'clock, just as we were sitting down for supper. It was a seductive, mournful sound, as mysterious as the nuns themselves, of whom we had rare glimpses as they moved about in fluttering white garments through their garden. The nuns were cloistered; garden and convent, a low white stucco building with a red tile roof, vaguely Spanish in design, were surrounded by walls. Having taken vows of poverty, chastity, and obedience, they lived austere lives.

It was rumored that they were often hungry, so Mother sent me with packages of food for them on holy days. Their door was usually unlocked. Once inside in the darkened foyer, one rang a little bell, a grill opened, and the package was received by invisible hands. A voice, altogether ethereal, expressed gratitude and offered to pray for any special intention. Such prayers were considered more efficacious than the prayers of ordinary nuns or even priests. I often attended Mass in their tiny white and gold chapel, hearing the soft rustling of garments behind a screen, the muted voices. So enticing then was the notion of absolute commitment, I thought that if I were to become a nun, I would become a Carmelite. The nuns at school were mainly Irish, visibly flesh and blood.

Sacred Heart School was located on Nelson Avenue across from the Noonan Plaza and those swans. English Gothic nestled up to art deco in the fanciful landscape of old Highbridge. The very structure of the school, certainly the name, established links to a different age and a different order of values. To a child's eye it took on the semblance of a medieval fortress complete with stone turrets, dark underground passages, narrow flights of stairs that came to an abrupt end, doors that were never opened. When I first attended, it was easy to imagine something faintly sinister lurking behind the walls or not too far underground. Something the nuns might resort to, perhaps, if you ventured in the wrong direction. They were insistent about direction—mental and moral and physical— all of which seemed concretized in the fact that our stone fortress was divided in two: one side for the girls, the other for the older boys. Some boundaries were more firmly fixed.

Boys were clearly a different species; culprits in school, a menace everywhere else. Smaller and faster guerilla fighters, their tactic was to hit hard and run. They battered us with snowballs, drenched us with water pistols, and broke up our games. The nuns treated them with scorn. In class they were restless, poor at penmanship, weak in grammar, untidy, furtive. For such crimes they were made to sit either in or under the wastebasket. The implications were apparent even then. Boys were relegated to a different, obviously inferior moral sphere that was somehow linked, in my mind at least, to pissing on street corners.

After the second grade they were banished to the other wing. And we were given to understand that if we ventured through the heavy doors that separated us from them, our souls would be in mortal peril. The boys had a separate schoolyard on the far side of the building and a separate entrance. As a further precaution, they came and went at different times, and so were only rarely glimpsed through the black iron mesh that divided the main staircase.

While the boys were taught by Christian Brothers in ways that were emphatic and direct, we remained in the tender hands of the Sisters of Mercy. Good manners were another aspect of "the right direction," the outward sign of God's grace along with white collars and cuffs and a neatly pressed uniform. Actually this didn't weigh too heavily on me. Nor did I mind at first the simple repetitive exercises through which everyone seemed to be learning how to read and write. On the whole these nuns were kindly, modestly educated women, who willingly tackled classes of fifty to sixty students. They were expert at handwriting and grammar and deportment as well as small domestic tasks like sewing, which they enjoyed themselves. Their expectations for us (as far as this world was concerned) were modest, too. There was no talk of professional careers beyond teaching or nursing. They didn't press us to enter the convent—that was a matter of grace, a rare thing. Most of us were expected to become good wives and the mothers of large families; there was perhaps more emphasis on the latter vocation. How this was to transpire remained a mystery. Perhaps at some point those heavy doors would swing open, and we would be permitted to meet the perfect Catholic husband, just waiting there in the corridor for the ultimate summons.

In my first year at school I underwent a transformation of character. I determined to be "Good," a novel concept given that I was much indulged as a small child, the first born in America. But the categories "Good" and "Bad" were firmly established by Sister Mary Magdalene, the most intimidating Sister of Mercy in the entire school. She was quick with praise, administered in the form of little colored stars and little pink slips stamped with the message "Good Girl," which I collected in a gold-papered cigar box. She was equally quick to punish, which meant a slap across the face, the wastebasket for the boys, and the back of the room for the girls. Anyone caught chewing gum had to wear it on her nose. Anyone caught talking during class had to scrub the blackboard after school. Even worse, she impressed upon us the idea that if she wasn't watching us, God was certainly doing so. Consequently there was no escape, no way of concealing our crimes. We had to confess the worst even if we were only thinking it. A bad thought was as bad as a bad deed. All this at the age of six!

Apart from moral values, though they seeped in here too, a hefty portion of class time in the early grades was devoted to handwriting. Most graduates of parochial schools can be distinguished by a clear handsome script. Not I. Not ever. All around me little girls bent over their desks, their pigtails stiff with determination, turning out rows of splendidly proportioned Rs, formidable Ts, eloquent Os. I sweated and sweated over the wrinkled sheets of my notebook but could master neither the straight line nor the elegant loop. Either my hand would falter or, when success beckoned with the last column, there would appear that fatal drop of Waterman's blue ink. And I would have to start all over again.

Matters were not made easier by the fact of ink. Pens invariably leaked onto clothes and books, no matter how careful I tried to be. Nor could boys resist dipping long, tempting pigtails into the inkwells on their desks. Blots materialized on white handkerchiefs and on homework that was all done. Writing had a certain romance to it before the advent of the ballpoint pen. One ventured stroke after stroke with deliberation, admiring the color, the irreversible nature of the process, the chance that the whole mighty undertaking would end in ruin.

If the subject matter was proving treacherous, my sister, Agnes, resorted to a novel tactic: She refused to attend class at all. Mother would take her to school by the hand and wave her through the entrance, but when she returned home Agnes, a true rebel, would be sitting on the doorstep. Any attempt to march her back down would be met with a violent vomiting fit and victory for my skinny sister. Mother would smooth over her absence, as she smoothed all conflicts with the nuns, by baking them a gargantuan Irish soda bread.

Normally our school day began promptly at half past eight as the principal, Sister Mary Margaret, mounted the school steps and rang her bell. We lined up silently class by class in the yard that formed a triangle between school and convent. The nuns, veiled in black with a white, crisply starched headpiece and bib, inspected us before the second bell rang and we were admitted to class. As long as we met their basic standards of neatness and cleanliness, we were okay. Our elbows might be fraying, the seat of our uniforms might shine. On these aberrations, they turned a less militant eye. But a girl without her uniform, like the girl in front of me without her underpants, was in trouble. She was sent home in disgrace or, worse yet, set apart from the others in class. Personal humiliation was a technique rarely used at Sacred Heart. While they wanted us to be their obedient children, most of these nuns had far better ways of managing us. After the first grade I certainly didn't fear them as they came and went from their convent, a small grey building with heavily curtained windows. In all my eight years there, I never got past the entranceway, which smelled of freshly baked bread.

The tidy corridors of our school were gaily decorated with posters as were all the classrooms along the second floor, which was the main floor of the school. The nuns greeted the seasons of the year with Celtic abandon. Their emblems were of the Earth, the changing colors reflected in our drawings and construction paper creations, our papier-mâché trees and pumpkins and stars. In spring tiny plants sprouted on classroom windowsills—sweet peas, poppies, nasturtiums. In October, Indian corn, acorns, and squash were gathered for display. They told us stories about Ichabod Crane and the headless horseman, and we read aloud passages from "Hiawatha," "Evangeline," "The Raven," and—a macabre touch—"The Cremation of Sam McGee" ("Then I up with his heels/ And smothered his squeals/In the scum of the boiling broth"). Christmas and Easter were, of course, the high liturgical seasons, prepared for by early Mass, with prayer and song, with pennies collected for the poor, and handmade presents. But at each turn of the year, holy day or holiday, there was a lifting of the heart, a celebration.

The nuns dominated our school life. There were no men whatsoever on our faculty and only two lay teachers. Mrs. Hersey, tall, red-haired, and jolly, taught art on Wednesdays. She wore long beads rattling on her bosom, carried a bulky string bag, and was very fond of purple. Squeezed in beside us, her bony knees flattened against the small desk, she could inspire the clumsiest fingers to draw an animal or turn a piece of construction paper into Napoleon's hat. She infused us all with an air of giddiness and pleasure, and at the conclusion of each lesson sprinkled us with chocolate kisses.

In many ways Mrs. Post was quite the reverse of Mrs. Hersey. She was a small, dark-haired woman in a Persian lamb coat—probably the only fur coat in Highbridge. Her specialty was math, and she covered the blackboards with rows of decimals and little bursts of algebra. Deeply concentrated, almost stern, she inspired the same behavior in us. No one ever strayed into the corridors from her class. Mrs. Post showed no interest in any student's work unless it was totally accurate. She gave us to understand that goodness was not the only criterion.

The only regular male visitor was our pastor, Monsignor Humphrey, who liked to drop by unexpectedly in his long black cassock, thrilling the good sisters and us alike. He always brought his dog, Rex. A handsome black St. Bernard, Rex took his turn up and down the aisle, inspecting our homework. He stood by knowingly while Monsignor quizzed us on the catechism. A kindly man, a true paterfamilias, balding, with a paunch and a liking for tobacco, Monsignor never embarrassed anyone. (He was also a safe bet in confession because he never assigned more than three Hail Marys as penance.) Praising such remarkable answers as he had received, he withdrew in a series of little flourishes, a ringed hand extended in blessing, curtsies from us, a gruff from Rex, the nuns smiling and pink with delight.

Though I went to school mainly to be with the other kids, I had only one or two close friends, who, unfortunately, lived at the other end of the parish. I seldom saw them outside school as our parents had little time for shepherding us back and forth. It probably didn't even occur to them that we might be lonely. Given strict orders to remain within calling distance, we were left to our own devices between school and suppertime. The only sanctioned alternative was the library, a white Dutch colonial building framed by trees that used to stand at the corner of 168th Street and Woodycrest Avenue.

That historic building, one of the original Andrew Carnegie libraries, has been unaccountably razed; in its place is something totally alien. I walked right past it recently, puzzled by what appeared to be a military bunker surrounded by iron fences, curving outward at the top and mounted with barbed wire. Flat, grey, faceless, it looked like something standing in a war zone. Groping around for the door, which was not easy to locate, I wondered whether the thing contained an arsenal or merely books. What child would be tempted to read here?

From the age of six to the age of eleven, I haunted the children's section of the original library, entered by a separate door, which contained small wooden chairs and tables on which one could spread out, as for a feast, illustrated volumes of fairy tales and folktales, myth and legend, tales of Rip Van Winkle, Robin Hood and Maid Marian, King Arthur and his knights. I always checked out the absolute maximum, like so many pieces of chocolate cake, astonished that it was all absolutely free and I could keep coming back for more.

Eventually—a triumphant day—I received a card to the adult section of the library and started in a fairly systematic way to read through the shelves of fiction. No one ever suggested *fact* to me. Starting with Jane Austen, I picked my way through names I had heard and through volumes that attracted my attention: the Brontë sisters, Thomas Hardy, Cervantes, Dickens, Mark Twain, Walter Scott, Sigrid Undset. A great favorite was *Wuthering Heights,* which I read over and over again, lured by the character of Heathcliff, doomed to a lonely, tormented life on a heathery moor. I suppose my notion of the ideal mate was fashioned after this proud and ferocious Heathcliff with his mysterious background, his spectacular suffering, and his undying love. Cathy's predicament—being fought over by two men—had its appeal, but she got out of the whole thing by dying. Hardly a route I wished to take. No, the real attraction was Heathcliff. (What yardstick did I have?)

Actually, I grew up in a home where books were treasured, stocked up, stuffed into bookcases, jammed into the upper reaches of our bedroom closet. I remember the feeling of absolute pleasure standing tiptoe on a ladder and stretching behind the stacks on the top shelf to discover something overlooked, something that had fallen into a crack, a treasure my father had added to the heap and forgotten. Only once do I remember any book being discarded; that was when Mother discovered *The Decameron* and hurled it down the dumbwaiter shaft, where it must have greatly astonished the person whose unfortunate task it was to haul out the trash.

In those days, despite a predilection for mystery and romance, I would read anything that fell into my hands—certainly comic books, which were forbidden as detrimental to morals and good sense. Alarmed by the prospect of censorship, I rigged up a communication system with Timmy O'Casey, a red-haired boy who lived upstairs with an older sister, Eileen. Being much overpowered by Eileen, he had a morbid turn to his personality and occasionally left a trail of iodine on the staircase, hoping we would take it for blood. Through him I was guaranteed a ready supply of sinister tales: *Reptile Man, Frankenstein, The Werewolf of Hill Hollow,* passed down by the simple expedient of a long string from the window above. (Mother always knew what was coming through the door.) So the long summer afternoons had their secret pleasures until she found me out and applied the flyswatter to my rear even as I reached out for the latest adventures of the Green Hornet. She had words for poor Timmy O'Casey, too, for corrupting me.

Although I grew up in a strict Irish household and was taught by Irish nuns, the pleasures of reading made me a confirmed cultural delinquent. I loved English novels, which in seventh grade were passed around the classroom like contraband. All the while I listened to tales and songs about Irish misfortune, my appetite for these novels grew. The American experience seemed raw. I liked stories about children named Lucy and Charles who addressed their parents as "Papa" and "Mum." I pictured them gathered around a cozy fire, a polished kettle on the hob, their buttered scones served up on a little tray with china cups. That was my idea of stability and bliss. Complete with a formal garden, little hedgerows, and a pony and trap. Thus I passed the time as the usual lessons on civics and grammar went forward. There was an odd truce between the monitors—five of us—and the nun in charge. We graded most of the tests, and in return we were pretty much left to ourselves in the back of the room. With fifty-five students, Sister Monica couldn't possibly get around to all of us, so she opted for the desperate cases.

The only time she became insistent was during the catechism recital: the nine beatitudes, the seven deadly sins, the cardinal virtues, the differences between mortal and venial sin. (Do they still exist?) There was no hope for it; we had to memorize the whole horrible litany because she would grade these tests herself. Furthermore, our principal made a point of visiting our classes specifically to check on our spiritual development.

We would be tested on all the spectacular virtues and vices, and she wanted us to shine. The only parts that were interesting, naturally, had to do with sexual sin. Phrases like "obscene thoughts and desires" or "occasions of sin" took on a lurid glow. These were perused feverishly in the hope of finding out more about what went on, what to expect, because parents and teachers maintained a monumental silence on the subject. The only concrete information we received was the usual muddled revelation from the tougher kids in the street. Language was so discreet in the old days; there were certainly no drawings on the lavatory walls or carved on the desks in parochial schools.

What was rape? I wanted to know. I also read avidly the worst stories in the *Daily News*. "Oh, don't worry about that," said Mother. "You'll understand all about that in due time." In due time! I was twelve! I could get pregnant. I knew plenty about my own biological system from a pamphlet she had thoughtfully provided, but beyond that I had scarcely a clue, nor it seemed did anyone else among my peers. That is, aside from Mary O'Reilly, a tall, giggly girl with hair like straw, whom no one took seriously until our pregraduation conference. There we were invited by one of the priests to ask any questions about sex we wished. No one had the nerve to raise her hand except for Mary O'Reilly. "Is French kissing a sin?" she wanted to know. "And is it a mortal sin, Father?" This led to amazing revelations about the properties of the tongue (another unforeseen moral precipice) and a new respect for Mary O'Reilly.

Apart from the properties of the sixth commandment, our curriculum in the upper grades was fairly dull. There was great emphasis on rote memory and on moral lessons gleaned from stories of emphatically good children. We approached the nations of the world through lists of exports, imports, minerals, mountain ranges, longest navigable rivers, and the like. History was important dates, the pros and cons of colonialism, the major causes of the Civil War, and the names of famous men.

Where were the famous women? They were saints, usually martyrs, torn to pieces by lions, toasted on grills, their bodies impaled, their breasts hacked off. Fully dismembered, they were infinitely pleasing to God. One beautiful saint prayed to God to save her from lascivious suitors. He answered with a skin disease so frightful that no man would come near her, for which she was grateful. What was the moral here? Clearly the bodies of women were suspect, in need of subjugation, chastisement, the rack. All of which I read with perverse pleasure, sometimes in school, sometimes in those little pamphlets that used to be found in the vestibule of the church. It was pretty hot stuff compared to Dick and Jane.

I think the particular genius of the Sisters of Mercy was to convince each of us of our immense spiritual value. Whatever our prospects as women—and I was only beginning to understand the implications here—we were all important in God's eye. They did not encourage competition or intellectual superiority. That was suspect. They had the usual Christian bias against science as being on the far side of a great divide, fundamentally alien to art and religion. There were certainly a few cranks among them, but most were spiritual democrats; decent, hardworking women. Everyone was expected to—and as far as I can remember, did—learn the fundamental skills of reading, writing, and arithmetic. Beyond that we were on our own. It bothered me terribly as I got older; classes were often repetitious, a waste of time. As a way of resisting the maternal coddling of the nuns, I expressed an interest in astronomy; the term had a fine heretical ring to it. I memorized distances in light-years, studied constellations and meteor charts, knew the diameter of the Earth and the phases of the moon. I took to name-dropping: "Cassiopeia," "nebulae," "corona borealis." Simple enough, but it set me apart from the potential teachers (God forbid!), the nurses, and the mothers of large families.

Despite the deadly regularity with which we were quizzed on the Baltimore catechism, all those lists of sins committed to memory, all that quibbling about limbo and purgatory and the unbaptized souls of infants, there was little talk of hellfire or the torments of the damned. The Joycean rite of passage came later. In grade school the nuns—apart from Sister Magdalene—regarded us as innocents, Heaven-bound, wreathed with ribbons of virginal blue. For our first Communion and confirmation we wore, not the discreet, anonymous robe of the present day, but the lacy veil and white dress of a diminutive bride. Afterwards I received from my parents a bouquet of roses and lilies of the valley and was photographed wearing a properly ethereal smile. Our link with the mysterious presence in the tabernacle, before which we knelt clasping white prayer books in white-gloved hands, was intimate and sure.

We were conscious at an early age of being part of an immense moral drama played out on a stage with celestial dimensions. Whole choirs of seraphim, fiery archangels, winged and bearing trumpets, were almost visible to our eyes. Whatever happened in the ordinary way as we labored at our desks or skated back and forth along the streets was just the tip of the iceberg, so to speak. If we had complaints, if we felt something lacking, that lack was in us, a failure of imagination, certainly of grace.

Dreaming away in the back of the classroom, I more or less accepted this view of things. When I felt restless, I never rebelled outright but escaped in the guise of a messenger, roaming the hall always with another message to deliver along another corridor. There were other refugees out there, delivering other such messages. As we kept up a respectable front, we got to spend considerable time together discussing the ways of God and man.

Just once the ways of man intruded, though we didn't at all understand the experience then. A young soldier appeared in the corridor where Catherine Cahill and I were idling away the afternoon. Cap in hand, he asked directions to the office of our principal, Sister Mary Margaret. Gazing steadfastly into his eyes, we politely obliged. Afterwards we admitted to one another what we had seen so oddly exposed through the neatly pressed trousers. We were filled with pity for him, angry with ourselves for having failed to warn him, failed in civility. How mortified he would be in front of Sister Mary Margaret.

DEATH'S DOMINION

On afternoons when we were children, Agnes and I often watched the footbridge in front of our house for the first glimpse of Father coming home from work—a signal to start up the tea and put the finishing touches on the supper. He walked briskly, a newspaper rolled up under his arm, bareheaded even in the rain. After eight or twelve hours in the subway, the walk was something he looked forward to. The fresh air and the quick momentum restored his energy, took the cramp out of his soul. I never understood how he endured that subway for thirty years, a man who loved the outdoors, whose mind was naturally quick and observant.

One day we waited with a letter from Ireland that contained news of his mother's death. We knew her only through stories and occasional letters, a card at Christmas. On his bureau was a blurred photograph of a heavyset woman in black, which seemed altogether unrelated to the woman who, we were told, loved to sing and play the accordion and invited children in to dance. Who was courted by a ten-year-old boy wearing his father's shoes and smoking his father's pipe. And who never forgave her one surviving son for abandoning the farm and going off to America. They had not seen each other in eighteen years.

It seemed a horrifying thing to me—then nine years old—to lose a mother, however remote in time and place. But what seemed even worse was that we would be the ones to tell him and thus be the immediate cause of his grief. Agnes and I stood at the window watching long before we knew he would appear on the bridge. We strained to catch a glimpse of him coming down the steps on the far side and watched him walk eagerly across and up the final flight of steps. Observing us at the window, he waved.

I still see him that way coming along cheerfully, not knowing what we knew. When he read the letter, all of us sitting solemnly in a row on one of the beds, Agnes and I cried. But he was not one to articulate his deepest feelings. In pain, he was simply silent. A religious man, and in certain ways opaque, he was not given to obtruding his emotions on the rest of us. He buried them out of long habit with the ghosts of his father and Michael and Ann and with the nameless little sister who had died of diphtheria. He believed that in God "all losses are restored and sorrows end." He fully expected St. Peter to meet him at the Eternal Gate. And he should have.

I have a map of Sligo drawn by him when he was more ill than we realized. Some of the details are blurred or inaccurate, but the fundamental direction is clear: "Take the road to Bundoran," that is, the road from Sligo town heading north along the sea to Donegal, a legendary signpost around which his old adventures seem to cluster. "Drumcliff, Yeats's country" is legibly inscribed. There is no indication of mileage; the turnoff is marked by a series of names interspersed with descriptive and cautionary notes: "Cloonabawn (Do this on a dry day, early. Don't drive in the rain or dark of night); Courtain Hill (good view of the ocean)." Next is "the Currys (two old men); Mary O'Brien (Irish Mary); and the Feighneys (Depend on what James Feighney tells you.)." The cross-hatching lines lead finally to "Cloonelly Lane," which is marked—for me as well as for him?—"You are home."

There was, of course, another sadness in the air during the war years of the 1940s. It came to me intermittently and was barely understood at first. There were terse, frightening radio bulletins: "the surrender of Corregidor," "another ship torpedoed," "fire out of control in London." The slogan "Remember Pearl Harbor!" echoed around us and was scrawled on walls and fences. There was a litany of terrible names: Midway, the Solomon Islands, Iwo Jima, Bataan. But in the newsreels Winston Churchill and Franklin Delano Roosevelt radiated optimism. Their powerful voices seemed consonant with our image of Uncle Sam, tall and determined in red, white, and blue. On University Avenue we collected mounds of fat, aluminum foil, and old newspapers, a community project into which we put considerable effort, lugging newspapers down to school in an old baby carriage. We were the home front, united behind "the boys overseas." We did without sugar, ate little meat, had "marge" instead of butter, planning meals around ration books. Down by the river under the High Bridge and in many backyards, victory gardens sprouted.

Black shades hung in the windows, and at night we obeyed the injunctions of the air raid warden patrolling the street below with helmet and flashlight. The buzz of an airplane propeller overhead, like the insistent call of "Lights out! Lights out!," seemed at the same time unreal and menacing, an association that remains with me still. As do the songs we played on the Victrola, learning them by heart as if they might provide us with clues as to what was really happening on the other side of the world. Much of this music was rousing and cheerful, assuring us that the "Yanks are coming" and the war would be won "over there." (No more patching up those rayon stockings!) But some of the music was hauntingly sad: "I'll Walk Alone," "I'll Be Home for Christmas," "When the Lights Go on Again." The adult world yawned again as a place of separation and loss. We saw Dana Andrews breaking his pilot's wings in *The Purple Heart,* choosing to die rather than betray his country. A celluloid image, but one that powerfully conveyed the heroism and sacrifice of the time.

No one we knew actually went to war, though there was considerable anxiety toward the end as men in their thirties—including Dad—were being called up and examined. What impressed me the most as I began reading the newspaper was the suffering of the victims. Details of the Bataan death march were horrifyingly vivid as were accounts of the emaciated Jews liberated from death camps and the scorched and shredded faces of Hiroshima. I read these stories over and over with dread and fascination, trying to understand what they meant. There seemed to be an undertow of misery and terror in the world that was never accounted for by anything I heard or knew.

One recent semester a Japanese student of mine wrote about the war. Her family had been evacuated to the countryside where her father, because of his age and position, was one of the few remaining men in the village where they were living. Toward the end the people went down every day to the train station to wait for the coffins of soldiers who had died at the front. The other children clustered around her father, and she remembered how jealous and resentful she was.

In Highbridge the fact of death was usually muffled by distance or the screen of fear concealing polio. Even then it seemed connected to that larger misery and terror that seeped in despite our prayers. Once, I saw a man climb quietly over the railing of the footbridge and jump, landing on the railway tracks alongside the river. He just vanished in the middle of the afternoon. Standing there, I was not altogether certain that anything had happened at all. A long time passed before the police siren began to wail and people gathered around the tracks. I never learned his name or anything about him. A total stranger, a thin man in short sleeves, passed along the steps where we were playing red light–green light, climbed over the railing, and died without a word.

Another death that haunted me for years was that of a little girl, whom I did not particularly like, who collapsed suddenly in the street. She was carried indoors, and we never saw her again. Patsy Ryan, with her round pimply face, black eyes, pug nose, willing to squabble with all comers, died from spinal meningitis. She came from a family troubled by misfortune and dogged by gossip. They did not conform to the pattern of life we knew because the parents had been divorced and the father subsequently shot himself. No one would actually say it was suicide. That was a terrible word. But the suggestion was in the air.

We were all a bit afraid of the mother, a thin, bony woman who often sat in the front window of her first-floor apartment, partly concealed by the drapes, watching the street. She rarely spoke and then only to ask us in a hoarse voice to play somewhere else. In a neighborhood of excitable, talkative Irish women, bursting with energy and self-importance, she was an anomaly. Cold, aloof, her white sharp features strained with tension and—did we imagine this?—a ferocity that might easily turn on us.

After her daughter's death she came outside. Dressed always in black, she grew noticeably larger, swollen. The contours of her face grew soft, the skin like putty. She took her place among the other women on the fence, sitting through the afternoons seemingly absorbed in the swinging momentum of their conversation. She was treated with deference and spoken to politely, if hesitantly, by the children on the block. She still inspired a kind of fear as though she had been marked by fate and might draw us along with her. She never seemed to leave the block, never made the little round of pious devotion that attracted her neighbors. I never saw her in a shop or at the bus stop. For me she remained always the very embodiment of grief, solitary, disfigured, inconsolable.

ROCKAWAY

My first holidays were spent at Rockaway Beach in one of the old-fashioned guest houses that used to line the avenues west of 116th Street. Coming from an apartment, I was charmed with the idea of a porch that creaked under your feet, that had rocking chairs, a large swing, and pots of geraniums. The landscape was vivid with color, and the air smelled of privet as well as the salty sea. Rows of white clamshells edged the driveway, and blue hydrangeas grew in the yard near the hose where we washed the sand off. The interior of the house made little impression. We only slept there. All our waking hours were spent on or near the beach.

Those early holidays were charged with glamour and unexpected largesse. We had beach balls in red, white, and blue, new pails and shovels, and an array of little shell-like scoops for digging in the sand. There were kites to assemble and fly, though there was always a great struggle with the tail, which was made by attaching strips of cloth to a long string. Too many and the kite collapsed; too few and it flew out of control. This was clearly an art in itself, as was keeping the string untangled as we played the kites out further and further along the shore.

Sand got into everything, into our sneakers and pajamas and hard-boiled eggs. As we usually ate on the beach, we came to expect sand with our sandwiches, washing it all down with hot strong tea. From my perspective, sand was irritating only inside my bathing suit, which now had the novelty of covering my womanly chest. After having her own formative years blighted by Irish weather, Mother was keen on sunning us as extensively as modestly allowed. Age seven was the turning point physically and spiritually. I acquired both moral responsibility—a dictate of the Church—and a top to my bathing suit—the dictate of my mother. The two developments were clearly connected.

The water was very clear at Rockaway in the 1940s, and little crabs flourished at the water's edge. We imprisoned them in sand castles until we left the beach at sundown and they were liberated with the tide. But sand with all its possibilities was a secondary source of interest. Our first choice was always to be in the water, and the rougher and wilder the surf, the better we liked it. Father taught us what he cheerfully termed "the dead man's float" as a safety measure, and then showed us the fundamentals of the crawl. After that it was hard to get us back to shore. I used to swim avidly out beyond the breakers and stay there, increasingly deaf and blind to any summons, my face a bright vermillion in the sun. Of course, if it was Father waving me in, this was risky. I could be beached for the afternoon. Now, lathering on the skin lotion (sunblock factor of thirty) and contemplating the fate of my epidermis, I groan. Little did we know back then about ultraviolet rays and the shrinking ozone layer. We swam until hunger or exhaustion propelled us shoreward.

I didn't even mind being tumbled head over heels by the incoming surf. There was a keen pleasure in the tugging violence of the water, in letting myself go with it, feeling it draw me down, and pitting my own strength and skill against it. Holding my breath until the point of balance was regained and I could surface. I was never afraid in the water though I knew very well that the sea was dangerous. There were drownings or near drownings every summer, and I had seen victims pulled to shore, including my own father, restored before I knew he was nearly lost. For reasons unclear to me then, it was the gathering ring of expectant, silent onlookers at the water's edge that was frightening. There was something more ominous, almost articulate, in their frozen stillness and patience than in the brisk sure motions of the lifeguards. Despite this I never feared the ocean. It gave me too much pleasure and, in an odd, exhilarating way, a sense of assurance.

In the evening we walked on the boardwalk down to 96th Street, my eye hopefully trained on the roller coaster, its bright spinning lights closer and closer on the horizon. But Playland with its gaudy and dizzying allure was not even a consideration as far as our parents were concerned. We were there for the natural advantages that the seashore had to offer. In daylight we swam and poached ourselves; in the evening we walked. If we could all manage two or three extra miles during the day, so much the better. Walking was less an exercise than a meditation. It was a release from the cramped compartments of city life, something our parents, coming from the West of Ireland, never got used to. It was time to re-assert the natural rhythms of the body moving freely through space. We were enjoined to look, to observe; the harmony of the universe was apparent only out-of-doors. Visiting a new place we paced all around it, felt it out with the soles of our feet. I still do this. A primitive impulse, I suppose, akin to the habits of certain animals marking a terrain with their own musky odors. Family walks also meant conversation. We talked out the events of the day, aired our grievances. Given a really fine walk, we became philosophical, expansive, heady with expectation. Walking fueled our optimism.

Years later as a teenager, after our summer home had been sold and a heavy discontent had settled over us, we went back to Rockaway for brief periods. As in our own neighborhood in the Bronx, here, too, many of the houses had become dilapidated. Now I was all too aware of dingy interiors, of the heat in the attic apartment which we rented, and of Mother's anger, which whirled around us, its current intermittent and unpredictable like the electric fan. We ate a lot of fried fish, and the ocean was still good for a swim, even late in the day after work. But it seemed colder and greyer than I remembered. There was debris in the streets. People and things looked shabby. We were shabby ourselves.

I took to walking along a canal lined with rusted barges and old boats, wondering where they had been, where they could possibly sail to now. Fishing from the docks, I discovered the canal was full of eels. Cold and voracious, they bit off my line, hook, and bait, and left me staring stupidly into the oil-slicked water.

The time of grace was early morning when I would go fasting and angelical to Mass, taking temporary leave of the world. And sundown on the boardwalk when the air was cool and fresh. Mother would talk about the farm she had lived on as a girl and forget about being a housewife in New York. We walked through the early evening hours, watching the lights twinkle on far out to sea and recovering a little of our old energy and expectation.

A GREEN WORLD

On the strength of a five-cent-an-hour raise, Father bought property and eventually built a summer house in Greenwood Lake, some forty miles from the city. It was a refuge from the hot summer streets, a benevolent green world, unquestionably an outpost of the country he had left behind. After the land had been cleared and a three-room house erected, he mounted a handsomely varnished, hand-carved sign with the name "Lissadell." A picture-book white, with green shutters and an apple tree, our house was situated at the end of a street entirely out of view of other homes in the area. A brook ran alongside, and beyond that was grassland with deer and an occasional long, black snake. Immediately across the way were blackberry bushes from which we made jam. For several years there was no electricity; in the evenings we turned up the kerosene lamp and lit candles. In the mornings we washed our faces with cold water and showered with a garden hose.

Constructing a house is never easy, particularly on a rock bottom budget. Father, however, was not a man to be discouraged. The subway had its specialists, he gave us to understand, men who were carpenters, bricklayers, plumbers, electricians. Men who knew insurance, men who knew cars. In times of mechanical breakdown and fiscal despair, we employed them. They saw us through the construction of our house, which took on the semblance of a family affair. Not wanting to lose any time while the sheetrock was being assembled, the paint applied, the tiling on the roof nailed down, Father worked with them, and they had meals with us at night. When construction was complete, it rained hard for several days, and we all waited for the weather to clear so the exterior painting could be done. The whole enterprise was nearly ruined when our murmuring brook suddenly roared over its banks right up to the back door.

Planking had to be rigged up so we could get around the yard and from the doorstep to dry land. Agnes and I went barefoot, hoping for fish, settling for frogs. Country life was even better than we'd expected.

As the elder daughter, from age nine to age fourteen I had plenty to do besides admiring our scenic isolation. The Protestant work ethic insidiously rooted itself in our Irish Catholic home. Row on loathsome row of vegetables had to be planted and—worst of all—weeded in the heat of the sun. Father, digging with pitchfork and shovel, turned a bristly acre into a grassy lawn. Agnes and I gathered the small stones for a garden path and weeded that lawn on hands and knees. The larger stones went to construct a wall alongside the brook. Little was wasted here either. Groceries were ferried home aboard my bicycle and every second day, because there was no refrigerator, I had to maneuver a large cake of ice along the two-mile road from the village. This was no easy task, particularly on the last stretch where a Doberman pinscher invariably waited for a piece of my anatomy. But my interest in maintaining the food supply—then as now—was always strong. And I liked the idea of pedaling off alone on a mighty and important task—Theseus against the Minotaur—which was rewarded with high praise and lemon cokes.

Journeying to Greenwood Lake was an adventure in itself. At first we had to tote the parcels and the suitcases, the cat, and the canary via subway to the Port Authority and there board a Trailways bus. Then, for one hundred dollars, Father made the momentous purchase of a 1936 Buick, only ten years old at the time. It had tasseled window shades, a grey velour interior, each well-upholstered seat with a commodious ashtray, and running boards. The body was a glossy black—no rust spots—polished weekly to a high shine.

From then on we went in style. It was the only car like it on the block, a fact which gave me pleasure but also some uneasiness. Was it desirable to have window shades? Here, too, I had no point of reference; none of our friends had cars. In the meantime we were mobile as never before, despite a certain cantankerousness about the motor (only six of the eight cylinders ever worked) and a little difficulty about the license. Crossing the mountain road along Route 17A into Greenwood Lake was no mean feat. Would we make it up the final hill? Would we be stopped by the police? When there was luggage, Father had to edge the Buick slowly over the top while the rest of us trailed him on foot. Then it was a freewheeling cruise, home free, to the bottom of the hill. I learned to drive the thing when I was fourteen or fifteen. It lasted for years, sputtering and coughing, the paint still gleaming. Shifting the gears was like operating a Trailways bus.

After a couple of years in which we photographed our house from every angle and lovingly planted rosebushes and lawn, our parents began to yearn for a fireplace. It was cold in the morning, cold in the middle of the night. And what is an Irish household without a hearth to roast potatoes and warm your shins at?

Another specialist arrived from the subway and went to work with Father early one June. Mother and Agnes were left behind in the Bronx while I was employed as cook and mixer of cement. I was enormously pleased with this elevation in status, a pioneer woman serving up vittles for the menfolk and one who had just escaped from school. I mixed that cement with gusto, toted bricks by the armful, and cooked earnestly. A totally new experience, of course, but I aimed to satisfy by quantity, producing well-toasted steaks and mounds of butter and potatoes. Skip the beans with their infernal stringy tips. To top it off there was MY-T-Fine chocolate pudding (my favorite) for dessert. Sawing cheerfully away at the food in front of them, the menfolk always looked grateful.

The chimney went up day by day, beautifully proportioned, a handsome, satisfying red brick. The fireplace itself was a marvel to look upon, though there was always a little problem about the draft. Our fires had a smoky quality, reminiscent of peat though less pungent, and no doubt good for the rheumatics. On cold mornings there was always a little bickering about who would put out a frosted toe and deal with the thing, but it was wonderfully pleasant in the evening when it rained and rained or the gas ran out, and we roasted dinner on the smoldering logs.

On rainy days we went fishing, mainly to have something to do but also because it was another way of pioneering, living off the land. The local pond was swarming with catfish and snapping turtles. We also fished for sunnies and small bass from the docks that jutted out onto the narrow neck of the lake, a mile from our house. There was always something to see from the docks, people in passing boats to talk to. There was the added drama of precariousness. The wood was rotting and occasionally gave way under our feet. I fell in once, dressed in my churchgoing taffeta skirt and Mary Jane shoes, and had to hike all the way home in plain and awful view along the highway, dripping and squishing at every step, tormented by the superior smile of Agnes, who never fell in.

For this episode I can think of no explanation. Normally we dressed in blue jeans and took our fishing seriously, hoping to come home with something truly astonishing at the end of our poles. The poles were homegrown, appropriately dried and stripped of the bark and fitted out with hook, line, bobbin, and sinker. We spent considerable time examining lures and hooks in the local hardware store which catered to fishermen. We hung around listening to them, debating the merits of the brightly colored flies, which we couldn't really afford though we had a nice collection of hooks. For bait we settled on leftovers from the kitchen and a copious supply of earthworms. The yard teemed with them. We captured them mercilessly and toted them in bucketfuls of soil to the docks, determined to complete the food chain. All this industry never produced a satisfactory meal that I can remember. Mother cheerfully cooked up the small fish we brought her, but they never tasted as good as we expected. Even the cat turned them down. For a while the big washbasin in the backyard teemed with the local catch. They were entertaining to observe, these denizens of my old nightmares swimming lazily around in the sunshine, but eventually we took to putting them back in the lake and then leaving them alone altogether. Hamburgers were better.

Thus we became accustomed to a life that moved in seasonal cycles between one landscape and another, like the ancient Irish moving their cattle to the high ground in summer. In the forties Greenwood Lake was an idyllic place with farms, orchards, and wide tracts of meadowland, a lush valley tucked in the hills with a deep, clear lake, seven miles long and teeming with fish. Our parents instinctively found a place there to invest with the values of the old country, so they could relive the habits and customs they held dear. They had to have a garden; the earth had to be turned over by hand, worked through stone by stone, taken possession of. When that was done, the hearth was lighted and we gathered in for the tea.

The extraordinary fact is that with all their past history of war, dislocation, and broken families, they created a secure and serene home for us, at least for a time—something I failed to do. Despite an awareness that I did not act alone and that I was young, inexperienced, and confused by the values of the fifties, I felt that failure, and my sons felt it. I dismantled my marriage to get away from a brutal, alcoholic husband and to free them from a bruising father. But, of course, we never did get away. The corrosive circle came round and round again.

After I had cancer, trying to find my way back to health and normalcy, I took to walking with a vengeance all summer long. I seemed to be walking simultaneously in two dimensions. The lovely winding paths through the Shawangunk Mountains converged with the roads I walked with my father in the summer evenings long ago. We used to turn off the main highway, the direct route to the village, and take the back road that wound down by the lake where we could see the boats and enjoy the gradual bend of the shoreline. As we passed over the bridge on the final stretch, there was a splendid view of the larger lake beyond. In the evenings swallows flew in circles over the bridge while below us the water swarmed with hungry fish. I loved to dawdle here, but Father would urge me to "step along, step along." We had different ways of walking. We both liked to try out all the side roads back and forth to the village, just to see what might turn up. He always stopped to inspect houses for sale and new construction sites, poking around knowingly at the lumber, speculating on the general layout of the house. Father had little patience with the merely scenic. He liked to walk rapidly with a purpose in mind: new understanding or a fresh supply of groceries. And as we walked, he told his stories or listened to mine, assembling in confidence our view of how the world fitted together.

The odd West of Ireland thing is that we were fairly isolated in Greenwood Lake. We kept to ourselves. Unlike the Bronx, there were few visitors here or close neighbors. I often felt lonely there in my early teens, which no doubt intensified a habit of introspection, encouraging me to see myself as an outsider. There were certainly other teenagers at the lake, a handsome, well-tanned, sociable, sexy crew. I hung around in their vicinity but had little luck in making contact. They seemed older in their ways, more knowing, less inhibited. I didn't twitch a muscle without considering its effect. I was uncertain how to dress, how to move, what to do with my hair. Hoping to appear stylish, I had my long hair cut and tightly permed with an effect that was bizarre as it grew out in a wavering friz.

I wandered all over Greenwood Lake, partially relishing my loneliness, biking along the back roads and out onto the scrubby peninsulas where boats were moored. I was crazy about boats and caught rides whenever I had a chance. I trespassed on the fringes of estates along the waterfront and sometimes, having nothing better to do, climbed a high fence to get out to Chapel Island, the site of a ruined church and the perfect spot for fitful melancholy. During the long afternoons I stayed submerged, swimming to the far side of the lake dotted with lily pads and thronged with amorous frogs.

Being at different awkward stages, Agnes and I were temporarily out of touch. She withdrew, clutching the cat, into a wigwam erected in the backyard. Each morning she would sweep out the bugs and twigs, thrashing the grass front and back for good measure, and settle in. She had her own secret projects. At home I levitated to higher altitudes like the fitful Irish poet, Sweeney in the trees. There were wonderful, dense oaks where I could roost in solitude, falling once or twice onto the barbed wire below. I also set up quarters in the attic, which required more dexterity as there was only sheetrock between the rafters, and a sudden slip would have sent me through the ceiling of the living room. There wasn't much air either, but the creative mind has other concerns. Here I brooded over my journals and performed minor experiments with potassium permanganate. Poetry I wrote ostentatiously, stretched out on the lawn.

Our parents never commented on this behavior. They were indulgent of studious, nerve-wracked types; what was one more eccentric in the family? Indeed, Mother encouraged me in patriotic and pastoral verse—"Through smoke and flame and cannon blast/the noble steed sped bold and fast"—responding with amazement at each burst of talent. She favored martial rhythms and rhymes that smacked their consonants together, qualities that went better with the patriotic genre. When Agnes was hospitalized with a frightening, severe viral infection, I penned a mournful poem on pink notepaper. "Patient sufferer"—I actually addressed her in this manner, bidding her to "arise!" and "dance." It went on in that vein for pages ("Mourn not for Adonis. . . . Ye caverns and ye forests, cease to moan!"), but fortunately did not precipitate a relapse.

Greenwood Lake was not like Shakespeare's green world where one discovers authentic values and then comes back to the city-court with a fresh moral perspective and a new ability to solve its problems. The country encouraged certain traits, a taste for solitude and independence, the need to make contact with the earth, to cultivate a garden. It nurtured us but did not send us back better equipped to deal with turmoil or pressure or change. It encouraged a need for inner space, for periodic flight and retreat, and deepened our nostalgia for the past. Family ties were strengthened, but in secret ways we began to rebel, to move apart from our parents and from each other, to crave, naturally, rooms of our own.

SONGS AND HORNPIPES

In an Irish household there is going to be music, much of it spontaneous and not always in the tradition. Father favored "The Soldier's Song" and something about violets and furs, delivered in a mild, tuneless baritone. Mother had a good ear and could quickly pick out a tune on an accordion or provide the chorus of a song: "Oh, young Rody MacCorly goes to die/on the bridge of Toome, today." She was also fond of ballads— "Only a Bird in a Gilded Cage"—that had to do with beautiful women who were rich and lonely or growing older.

We had a well-worn collection of records featuring the likes of John McCormack, Morton Downey, and Dennis Day, which were played on a massive mahogany Victrola after a great thumping and cranking of the arm. "O Danny Boy," "The Last Rose of Summer," "The Harp that Once Through Tara's Halls" provided a plaintive background to family conversation, reminding us of all the men who had died and the hearts that were broken for the lost, fair land of Kathleen Mavoureen. The lovers trailing to the "pure crystal fountain" sounded as mournful as poor Kevin Barry climbing "the gallows tree." I couldn't get enough of it. The songs worked a kind of enchantment. It was the family story over and over in a new guise, to be swallowed gulp after gulp with strong tea. And to tell the truth, although my ear has been tuned to the old Gaelic music, I still love those sentimental melodies, Moore's Maladies, along with the harp and shamrocks, wolfhound and round tower.

As soon as I could hum a few bars, I was instructed to take myself seriously as a singer, an important asset to the household. On festive occasions after a suitable humming and hawing, I was bustled forth to sing for the company in a style modeled on the voice of the Victrola. Such tumultuous applause as I received led me to extend my repertoire with various gems garnered from books Dad had stashed around the apartment. "Flow Gently Sweet Afton" was a real showstopper. Having no idea how this stuff was supposed to sound, I invented a maudlin tune and delivered it in a striking attitude, head thrown back, hands pumping the air. The family thereupon determined I was ready for professional training.

A vocal teacher was secured, a blonde bosomy thrush, who proffered me a pitch pipe and a lush collection of ballads: "Thine Alone," "Embraceable You," "The Anniversary Waltz." We sang them together in swooning duets. More treats for Agnes, to say nothing of the neighbors.

As little was concealed in our apartment dwelling, when an accordion sounded or a voice was raised in song, all were compelled to listen. They might knock on the pipes or send up a chorus from the street, but the artists in residence were not easily stifled. There was always music in the Bronx. On holidays—mainly Halloween and Thanksgiving—scores of children would troop through the alleyways singing at the top of their lungs. The odd fiddler might come through any day of the week. Neighbors would respond by tossing coins—and an occasional bucket of water—from the windows. Thus were the arts encouraged at the local level. Unfortunately, my parents became ambitious, encouraging me to try out for television shows and to take part in little musicals and minor entertainments. I was being groomed for *Ted Mack's Amateur Hour,* although I didn't have the nerves for it, being affected in a most unpredictable way by stage fright. At times a thorough ham, I enjoyed performing in public; other times I sweated profusely and lost the pitch or the place and all my composure.

The one occasion that caused me no trouble whatsoever was the Irish Feis, a gathering at Fordham University every spring that offered traditional music, dancing, sports, and rhetoric. Prizes were offered for the outstanding competitors in each category. In earlier years Agnes and I were decked out in gorgeous bunting—white silky blouses, green pleated skirts, ribbons in our hair, and a large placard with entry numbers pinned to our heaving little chests. We were two among the long lines of eager dancers, each climbing in turn to a platform to perform one step of a jig or reel or hornpipe for the ecstatic multitudes. No one expected ei-

ther of us to win anything; the important thing was to be there to partic-
ipate in this celebration of Irishry.

We were trained for the grand affair by a "Professor" McKenna, an
exacting dance master, very nimble himself and quick to poke ungainly
legs with his blackthorn stick. He went for the high leaps and the deftly
executed turn, arms pinned to the side, movement only from the waist
down. I never quite mastered it, but Agnes showed promise and was not
at all put off by the temper of McKenna. She danced all the more lightly
to the tempo of his explosions, the crack of the stick, the squeal of the fiddler. She had a temper herself and knew his was mostly sham.

At some point Professor McKenna vanished from our lives. Although
we continued to dance on festive occasions the same steps over and over,
we were clearly out of the running until, that is, new talents asserted
themselves: rhetoric and song. So we went to the Feis, no longer little innocents in green bunting but eager for approval, or at least I was, under
the suddenly judgmental eye of Father. Would I measure up after all those
voice lessons, which involved some sacrifice, considering his modest
salary?

While Agnes maintained the family honor with the words of the
"bould" Robert Emmet ("When Ireland shall take her place among the
nations of the world"), I sang traditional airs accompanied by an Irish
harp. In the middle of a dense, exhilarated crowd, I was wholly unself-
conscious and happy, floating on the surface of the music. Afterwards we
were feted with icy ginger ale, spicy ham sandwiches, whatever we
wanted. We listened to the skreel of bagpipes and basked in sunny approval. The only letdown came the day I failed to win a gold medal.
There was no talking to Father on the drive home along University Avenue. He maintained an angry, intimidating silence, chided by Mother,
but for once unresponsive. It took a minor collision to alter his mood.
Perhaps the second canceled out the first misfortune. He expostulated
heatedly with the other driver, pounding the roof of the car. It was all
right. No one was hurt. "For God's sake, Dan, let's go home and forget
about it," Mother pleaded. It was a rare show of temper and of disappointment. Father's expectations were largely unspoken or spoken only
indirectly. He was a modest man and a subtle one. But you knew he had
plans for his daughters.

For all its Irish associations, music provided a link with the world outside the Bronx. At thirteen I found a new teacher, Mrs. Baumgarten, a well-upholstered woman with a buttery contralto voice. Her four-room apartment, swathed in grey velour and lit softly by long drooping fringed lamps, held two grand pianos along with a husband and a grown son, who kept a discreet distance. She introduced me to lieder, to the music of Bizet, Hoffmann, Schubert, Jerome Kern. She taught me to breathe "from the diaphragm," gave me a smattering of German and French, and led exercises "to bring the voice forward": "meee, maaay, maaah, moooo, muuuu" in ever-ascending halftones. I would have happily gone on visiting her once a week for the rest of my life, biking down University Avenue to 162nd Street with a pound of music under my arm.

I had no professional ambition; as I grew older, my competitive instincts weakened. Despite my parents' hopes, music was not connected in my mind with the workaday world. I was a shy singer, although not altogether willing to blend into a chorus. I liked to sing the high counterpart, to pitch my voice into the nave of a church or the back of an auditorium and fill it with sound. It seemed to me, being of a secretly religious nature, a kind of prayer. But, more than that—confess it—music gave me a sense of power and delight.

Each year there was a recital in the concert hall downtown for which we were carefully coached and over which Mrs. Baumgarten presided in a snug, glittering gown. One spring we produced *Hansel and Gretel,* which necessitated weekly ventures with two friends to a dance studio in "the city." We had been given gloriously idiotic roles as "sprites" complete with wings of buckram, homemade gowns, and little sacks of rose petals. It was decided that we required coaching to move airily, strewing our petals over the pathetic children who had the good roles.

In the Manhattan studio we mixed with real dancers and actors; handsome, exotic, and skinny, smoking cigarettes and talking openly about work and sex in the theater. The experience didn't inspire me to throw my lot in with them, although I loved all the melodrama and seductiveness they exuded. I think I was mainly impressed with the way they built up distinctive characters for themselves and made a point of looking as little as possible like anyone else. In school we were encouraged to smooth down any rough edges, to tune continually to common concerns. We were supposed to be modest, polite, and self-effacing, to be little nuns, I presume. It took an effort to be rude and self-assertive, two modes of behavior so oddly equated.

Singing as a soprano has been compared to flight, soaring, becoming ethereal. I remember vividly that pull of the ethereal. I can't frame the experience any other way. That voice is lost to me now, but the instincts of the soprano are still there. I like to sing, and each time with the impulse comes the desire to pitch my notes to the higher keys, to leap free.

What I have instead is a deep alto sound, oddly enough, the sound of a cabaret singer or a blues singer craving one more for the road. Singing in this voice is like managing an awkward rubbery sort of garment. It doesn't fit right or feel right, but I can't send it back. So I try to make it fit, get a grip on it, trim the rough seams.

A soprano voice is pitched up and forward through the nasal passages; one concentrates on loosening the jaw and vibrating columns of air forward and backward toward the ear. I struggle to project this strange new voice down through the belly until it vibrates in the gut, or seems to. Getting the vocal cords to vibrate at the right pitch is a matter of placement. It's a peculiar sensation and even a pleasurable one, getting further down into the body, getting comfortable with it.

THE FLESH AND THE DEVIL

Peering out from under her sunbonnet in old photos, two-year-old Agnes looks wistful. She had realized—now she tells me—that she looked like Winston Churchill.

A good self-image was not something either of us acquired easily, although Mother did her best for us. As soon as Agnes's hair was long enough, she went to work on hers as well as mine, rolling it up each night in rags—how did we ever sleep?—to produce that bouncing, sausage-shaped, Shirley Temple effect so much in vogue. We knew our souls were in mint condition, bright and glittering although vague in detail. (Did souls have eyes?) We kept them that way by a continual round of devotions: Mass on Sundays and holy days, rosaries, novenas, stations of the cross, little acts of self-denial. No candy in Lent; no meat on Fridays.

We seemed then to have a measure of control over this spiritual dimension that was reassuring, but the physical self was ornery, unpredictable, inclined to develop pimples and to grow in spurts.

Menstruation didn't bring us any marvelous new sense of womanliness; if anything we became more acutely self-conscious than before. The important thing impressed on us from every side was to conceal the whole messy business as much as possible. Neutralize it. Don't talk about it. If you passed out in school, you were "feeling a little unwell." A curtain of euphemisms was pinned around us. The nuns were extremely kind about our "little weaknesses." Yet there was no avoiding the feeling of disgrace when Mother arrived in a flurry of whispers to take us home.

Time and again we were reminded that women brought forth their children in pain and sorrow. After childbirth they were purified, received meekly back into the church, praying with a lighted candle at the foot of the altar. Women were all too directly connected with blood and original sin, all the ills that flesh is heir to. So much of what was taught denied the truth of Yeats's paradigm: The body had to be "bruised to pleasure soul." In the church we attended, images of the crucifixion and of saints being burned or flayed alive were prominently displayed, openly celebrated. On Good Friday a life-size effigy of the mutilated Christ, crowned with thorns, the side pierced and bloody, was kissed fervently by the faithful, who stood in long lines down the central aisle of the church.

No wonder I began to feel guilty.

There seemed to be a system of checks and balances operating when I was a child. If I did something wrong, I was forgiven, providing I confessed and mended my ways. But as an adolescent I did things I never intended to do, got caught in accidents and misjudgments that never seemed to get straightened out or separated into the neat mortal and venial categories that concerned the nuns. No matter how hard I tried there was an unaccountable slippage.

"I'm the boy whose leg you broke." It was not an accusation, exactly, more like an affirmation of our relationship in case I hadn't recognized him, a bow-legged, freckled eight-year-old with an engaging grin. No hard feelings that I can detect. As though my slamming into him with my bicycle, when he ran out suddenly into the street, were a phenomenon of nature. He walked away from the accident quite steadily, me following with apologies, fearful that I had inflicted some hidden injury. Which indeed I had.

When we met two days later, his attitude was much the same, sturdily cheerful, with perhaps a hint of a swagger in the way he maneuvered his left leg—the one with the cast—along the street. He seemed as active and talkative as usual, scarcely troubled by his condition.

It was his habit in the years that followed to knock occasionally on our door or appear in the middle of a curbside conversation. Not abruptly, just matter-of-factly, to observe without any particular emotional force: "I'm the boy whose leg you broke." And I would be overwhelmed by misery and guilt, to say nothing of the conviction that any witness to this event would henceforth regard me as a monster. Perhaps the boy was waiting for me to explain why I had hurt him, thinking that older kids had solid reasons for what they did. Perhaps he only wanted another ice cream cone. I came to think of him as a little ghost—like Bartleby—my own personal victim, whom I would never assuage because he was never angry.

As a teenager I began to suspect that my fate was a murky one. This impression was, of course, intensified by Christian emphasis on the treachery of Eve. The priests at Sacred Heart were moderate men who sighed with relief when they ended the sermon and could offer the blessing. But the missionaries who presided over annual retreats at our parish church and in high school were in league with Torquemada. They roared from the pulpit, summoning up visions of hellfire and eternal suffering reserved for those guilty of "impurity" (that is, those with sexual impulses). By a curious twist of logic, women (the weaker vessels?) had a responsibility to set the proper example and keep the men at bay. Virginity was our greatest treasure, "a bright jewel," so precious to God that we should be ready to die rather than yield it up (without permission from the Church). When I finally read *A Portrait of the Artist,* that Jesuitical sermon was all too familiar as was the terror it inspired in poor Stephen Dedalus.

The more I learned, the more nervous and guilty I became, particularly under the questioning of priests in confession—this was before Vatican II. "Bless me, Father, for I have sinned." "And did you sin in thought or in deed? Alone or with others? How many times? And are you truly sorry, my child?" I was treading on moral quicksand. Every motive seemed to harbor yet another deeper, more sinister motive. Even the act of examining such motives was open to question: Was I being overly scrupulous, a sin in itself? But to stay a long time in the confessional box puzzling over these matters was a dead giveaway. Everyone would know you were mired in sin or sex: The two were for a time synonymous.

By temperament I was given to extremes. I could never follow the example of my Irish mother who took exactly what she wanted from the Church. She enjoyed the rituals, attended Mass and all the special services with devotion, but never allowed any dogma of the Church to interfere with her way of thinking. Intent on her rosary, she scarcely listened to the priests, although she would comment favorably on the fiery rhetoric of the Passion fathers. In her secret heart she ascribed to God the true virtue of common sense.

Despite the risk of damnation, I had the usual romantic fantasies at the usual time in life. Perhaps they were made more intense (Allan Bloom's hypothesis?) and lasted years longer because of fear and uncertainty, to say nothing of the physical barriers erected by priests and nuns. The male adolescent to my inexperienced eye was a creature of alien appetites—inscrutable, speaking a different language, ripe for intrigue. He was in no way related to the little creeps who chased after us in earlier days.

My thirteen-year-old fantasies swarmed around a muscular boy who sang in the choir, served Mass on Sundays, and owned a collie. We made eye contact during the benediction. He had a pleasantly sophisticated quality, signaled by an angular Scandinavian profile and an occasional book under his arm. Always on the move away from "the block," where most of us spent our afternoons, he seemed to possess a secret, separate life, he and that dog.

In my diary, which alas did not possess a lock and key, I took to jotting details of near encounters: "April 5. Saw J.M. at Mundinger's deli. He likes mustard and sauerkraut." "April 9. Saw Him crossing Ogden Ave. with Lad. Looked friendly." Eventually, having little to report and little else to do in class, I took to embellishing these scenes: "April 20. Met J. this evening on Brown's Hill. His hair was ruffled in the wind. Without a word, he embraced me feverishly." "May 2. Feeling his hot breath on my cheek, his fingers reaching for the delicate lace at my throat, I trembled, etc., etc."

One day, their curiosity aroused by this new habit of writing, my classmates made off with the diary, reading it back to me in fragments—with emphasis on "hot breath," "ruffled hair," and "trembling"—all through the long weeks that were left in the term. Portions of the diary turned up in notes that went back and forth in school. Other portions were delivered in a mocking chorus on street corners. They knew well enough that my seduction theme was pure fiction; that made it entertaining. Had they believed me at all, they would have gone into shock and spoken in whispers. As it was, nothing I could do, either hiding or brazening it out, would stop them. They had discovered the power of rhetoric; I had discovered the peril.

This season of misery blew away unexpectedly. Rumor must have reached the object of my passion because he invited me—a definite date, my very first—to the eighth-grade prom. The diary was never mentioned, and in the face of this undeniable achievement my tormentors withdrew. J.M. brought me a corsage of roses, which was pinned to the shoulder of my pretty white eyelet dress and then nestled in a scrapbook for years. At the parish hall, where he escorted me promptly at eight o'clock, we did not dance together. The style then was to mill around in little smiling clusters. Indeed we smiled a great deal, all of us too timid to approach the Great Mystery, but thrilled to feel it close at hand.

After the great coup of the prom, our romance took a desultory turn. We went to separate schools for separate sexes and for a while, both cursed with the need for indirection, went about in a group of four, each of us paired with a different, more assertive partner. So much for the entanglements of early adolescence which I remember, after the pleasing bloom of thirteen, as being a period of acute physical awkwardness and hideous clothes, secondhand dresses, coats too short, sweaters too large, everything a bit wrong somewhere.

Contact with the opposite sex was fleeting and strange. We spoke in formulas, insults, dopey remarks. "Luckies? Yeah! Don't smoke anything else." ("Yeah.") We spent a lot of time trailing one another around town, gazing across fences. When I got closer, I felt I was tiptoeing through land mines. They sometimes exploded in my head.

There were all those gradations of sin worsening and worsening with the pressure of a male hand. To say nothing of those venial kisses spiraling into mortal sin. How would I explaining it in confession? If I died suddenly I would end up in Hell singed to a crisp.

The basic facts were still hard to come by. Adults provided ample warning, but little useful information. My source of enlightenment was the aseptic diagrams in biology texts, which I read furtively in library corners. I wouldn't want anyone to think I had an unnatural interest in the subject.

I had no idea how to begin a flirtation or possibly thought it was base behavior. I never went up to a boy directly, but maneuvered my way onto the path he was likely to take. Day after day I would wait for a phone call, never daring to pick up the phone myself. A seesawing mouse keen on adventure, I was afraid of falling short of that model of purity and propriety so firmly implanted by the nuns. A direct approach might consign me in the mind of the equally confused Catholic male to the ranks of fallen women.

After my Nordic hero locked himself in with the Christian Brothers (a secret life, indeed), I took notice of a family with four boys living two floors down. Here, I could conveniently focus my energies. I began by idolizing the eldest and tallest, a stern, intellectual-looking boy, who went off to a seminary without noticing me at all. The odds against Irish Catholic girls used to be formidable. Heartsick, but still game, I shifted attention to the next one, a shaggy football player whom I had spotted slipping out of Mass before the last gospel. I used all my cunning to ensure that our paths would frequently cross. I rooted with abandon at football games. I befriended his mother. To no avail. Possibly I was expecting an epiphany of some sort. One morning as I was lurking on the staircase, ostensibly waiting for the mailman, there would be a sudden shaft of light, and he would recognize the desirable woman inside those baggy jeans.

When it was clear that he had fallen for a vulgar girl who looked like Elizabeth Taylor (and probably never even went to football games), I began with faint hope to bump into the third brother, sixteen at the time, humorous and thin. And willing to say hello. What to do next? I racked my brains—the first mistake, of course. Where were my instincts? All I could manage was some awful Byzantine remark. I didn't have the courage (or the eyelashes) to try for that wide-eyed, melting expression I had observed in the movies. At fourteen or fifteen, like the dreamer in "Araby," I was doomed to hunger in the distance. The youngest was really too young; I had met him once too often being chased along the streets by his mother, a fierce Kerry woman waving a broomstick, determined to keep those "buoys" in line.

For a while I thought of taking up religion myself.

INTEMPERATE NEED

Sister Monica was a fairly demented nun, probably in her fifties, though it was hard to tell about nuns. Hard-pressed to maintain control as she careened along from math through civics to grammar, she forced rebellious cases to their knees before the class or else consigned them to the clothes closet. One culprit was incarcerated for two weeks, desk and all, her voice muffled and resentful among the winter coats. Eventually she got around to me, but when I refused to budge, she let me alone. It was a rare gesture on my part, meeting her head on instead of rapidly shifting ground and locating a detour.

Apart from occasional bursts of spleen, we got along amiably enough in the eighth grade. Sister Monica called us "her girls" and posed toothily alongside us for photos. And she inscribed her name among the little poems and epigrams we were collecting in autograph books we expected to keep forever. ("Rocks and rills divide us/Distance be our lot/You may have forgotten me/But I'll forget you not.") For my own part I scarcely listened in class, escaping as usual into the hallways or lost on the Egdon heath with Eustacia Vye. I was consciously drifting through the days, anticipating high school. Meanwhile it was not unpleasant reading novels and daydreaming in the back of the room, a lopsided education, no doubt, but one which shaped my moral sense as much as did the Baltimore catechism or my parents' earnest example. Heroic self-sacrifice, alone and misunderstood (though not indefinitely), like Sidney Carton in *A Tale of Two Cities* mounting the guillotine, had enormous appeal.

Tethered within the congenial circle of our parish, most of us were uncertain about choosing a high school; there wasn't one in Highbridge. The main thing impressed upon us was that the school should be a Catholic one where we would be "safe," where our religious beliefs would not be questioned. Indeed, after nearly eight years among little girls with blue ribbons on their pigtails and rosary beads in their pockets, we were afraid of the public schools. The kids looked tough and intimidating and slick. You only went there if you couldn't afford Catholic school tuition (fifteen dollars a month in those days plus the cost of uniform, books, and transportation).

This precipitated a crisis at home, and there was considerable pressure on me—the intellectual—to win a scholarship. So I was sent one day into Manhattan for the examinations at a large diocesan school, one I had actually seen and which struck me as the fifties equivalent of Dickens's bootblacking factory. Instead of getting off at midtown, I spent the morning riding the IRT with a few cronies who had similar reservations, seeing how far we could travel on a nickel. So much for noble self-sacrifice. While my poor, trusting parents waited hopefully for word from the school, I skulked around the house, never admitting my guilt. What made it even worse was that they never voiced their disappointment, thinking I had done my best.

Eventually they sent me off to Aquinas High in the East Bronx, which had a reputation for music. It was the only thing that reconciled me to their uniform, which was remarkable even in those days. The blue jumper and white blouse were designed to produce a figure more rectangular than curved. But these were familiar items as was the white beret (easily tucked in a pocket out of sight). Much more formidable were the dress blue cape lined with gold and the stout oxford shoes—white for special occasions. In that getup, it was impossible to blend in with the crowd, which was, of course, the point. You were immediately identifiable standing on a street corner or marching in a parade along Fifth Avenue, a phalanx of Aquinites trained to step snappily, military style. We were always on parade, so to speak, and thus expected to be paragons of Catholic virtue and civic responsibility. It was a shock to discover that at this school even minor vices, chewing gum or wearing makeup, were penalized: "You are a disgrace to your uniform." How did so many nuns become enamored of West Point? For smoking a cigarette you were, figuratively speaking, placed in the stocks for weeks, a fallen woman with a giant C embroidered on your bosom. Your parents had to beg them not to expel you. At first I was so intimidated by the ferocious barrage with which minor infractions of the rules were treated that I scarcely imagined bolder enterprises. The Sisters of Mercy had regarded us as little innocents; the Dominicans took a postlapsarian view.

The Mother Superior inspired terror in our ranks; even as seniors, we felt our knees tremble when she spoke. She questioned us with an air of open suspicion, always expecting, it seemed, the worst sort of motive for our behavior. Her voice and figure were large and her temper uncertain. Even when she congratulated me on some little achievement, she made me nervous. I felt oddly guilty as if through the powerful lenses of her steel-framed glasses all my sins were visible. Part of her effectiveness derived from her manner of appearing only rarely and then very abruptly. She took you by surprise, and all you could do was to look neutral and slide out of sight, desperately hoping to avoid her interest. Other sisters established the daily routine, taught classes, presided over meetings. She operated mainly behind closed doors, a dynamo generating the moral force upon which the school depended.

After enjoying senior status in the eighth grade as well as the admiration of all the little tots, we were reduced to trembling freshmen. Green and foolish, we stood in line in the auditorium as our names were called out one by one, and we were allocated a minor niche in the scheme of things. We were weighed down by the baggage of learning, each textbook papered and labeled, each notebook arranged in tiers, appropriately marked, along with graph paper, ruler, compass, pens, and pencils of an exact grade and type. All were secured in a large book bag, also labeled; nothing was left to chance. Each morning we assembled at the bus stop with book bags and bus passes in hand, promptly at 7:45. Shined and pressed in blue, white, and gold, we were prepared to dazzle ordinary commuters along the route to Aquinas High.

Of course this place had no boys in it either. Within the snug enclosure of Aquinas, our adventures were to be intellectual and spiritual ones. Chastity was daily extolled as a virtue; a life of celibacy was an exemplary life. Nor were boys ever mentioned in class except under the rubric "occasion of sin." Males were fathers or historic figures or members of the clergy. The rest were repressed, which of course intensified the mystery and the Heathcliff syndrome. Even in our famous musicals, male roles were played by us little women. The romantic lead was a tall classmate dressed in velvet tights, sporting a Woolworth's mustache. Shakespeare in reverse. Parents, as you might expect, were enthusiastic about the value of concentrating on studies without the distraction of a male element.

In class in the absence of a male or a secular perspective, we sharpened our wits against the nuns. But the terms were usually their terms, and no matter how much they might seem to give way, one could sense them knitting us firmly into the fabric of their belief, snugly enclosing us in a world whose rituals were sacred and solemn and often very beautiful.

They were at their best in the Christmas season when classes dissolved into singing sessions, homework assignments were forgotten, and the school throbbed with festivity and expectation. The crankiest among them—and that was certainly the typing teacher—visibly brightened and purred at us all through the drill. She was determined to make good secretaries out of us and had reason to despair.

The high point of the season was Midnight Mass at the old people's home nearby. What might seem at first a dreary prospect, dragging us away from a warm bed and a sparkling tree, was in fact very moving and splendid in its way. We traveled in the frosty dark, lightheaded with fasting and pleasure at being abroad at a strange hour, to sing the Bach B Minor Mass. A Midnight Mass, chanted in Latin in a tiny candlelit chapel, for which we had practiced for weeks. The celebrant was our chaplain, garbed in white and gold, familiar and solemn, as he intoned the opening prayer, *"Introibo ad altare Dei,"* and we sang out the response, *"Ad Deum qui laetificat juventutem meam."* The service was eerie in its concentration. In that darkened space, above the listening but invisible congregation, we seemed a great distance from the ordinary world. As the lovely old music swelled in exaltation—*"Kyrie eleison . . . Christe eliyson"*—it was not hard to imagine a flock of cherubim joining in the chorus. The only discordant moment came with the opening bars of *The Confiteor* as I waited to sing a cappella the central, sacred passage: *"Et incarnatus est de Spiritu Sancto ex Maria Virgine."* After a fierce nod from our choir director, it was like leaping into midair. Had I missed the notes, I would have gone home in despair, the holiday in ruins. To sing them perfectly was to come closest in my mind to the ritual enacted by the priest. It was a moment of true grace. At the close as the old people left their pews, we sang traditional carols, sending them away, we hoped, a little happier than before.

Many of the nuns who taught us, including our choir director, were distinctive and compelling in character. Indeed we spent considerable time scrutinizing them; their behavior was an inexhaustible topic of concern. Unlike the Sisters of Mercy, whom as children we more or less took for granted, these Dominicans never appeared to be ordinary women, but to have another dimension, impenetrable and powerful. They were the chosen, bound by awesome vows, the Brides of Christ. Thus their words, their moods, their little tirades were more fascinating to us than most other things we studied. We tried to imagine them without their habits, their stiff white linen, the heavy beads and crosses that swung from their waists. Did nuns have legs? Never mind hair on their heads or anywhere else.

In a curious, paradoxical way, they encouraged independence. There were certainly humble and cheerful souls among them, but not a few were as proud and authoritative as any Jesuit and equally unswerving in their mission of educating us. My Latin and math teachers, rigorous and smart, made us work long, solitary hours on their assignments. They were very different in manner. Sister Helena was gentle, diminutive, infinitely patient, and generous with her time. She had a will of iron commanding conjugations and declensions, but also a wholly romantic vision of Europe to inspire us. She had always wanted to see Mont-Saint-Michel and the castles on the Rhine.

Sister Immaculata had no patience whatsoever. When a foolish hand went up, she visibly struggled for charity, becoming fiercely red and violent about the eye. The chalk would snap, and she would pound her chest, trying to speak calmly. There was one poor girl, feeble in trigonometry, who had only to look away from her text to bring the lesson to a shuddering halt. Sister Immaculata would pray aloud for patience; the culprit would sink into her desk, and we would all wait breathlessly while the drama worked its way to the usual conclusion: paralysis on the one side, heroic endeavor on the other. Like my old friend and math teacher, Mrs. Post, she rarely praised good work. She simply expected it as the usual state of things, which suited me entirely. I didn't wish to be noticed at all, having developed the full-blown neurosis of adolescence, alternately very outspoken and miserably shy, unable to string six words together without a nervous breakdown. It was a relief to work out quirky formulas in algebra or trigonometry, to find the correct solution to something in life.

Religion and English and science were tedious. In religion we recited the rosary, purchased bricks for churches in Ecuador and Chile, and memorized elaborate lists of virtues and divine attributes. Even sin was made to seem dull. The same approach was used in chemistry: There was little theory and much rote memory work. I avoided biology, not wanting to do anything to the organs of frogs, and took out my hostilities on the poor, meek, Spanish instructor, who was not a nun.

It was English that was the real disappointment. Here I was expecting something. The list of authors was wonderful: Shakespeare, Keats, Wordsworth, George Eliot, Walter Scott. . . . But the emphasis in class was invariably and ploddingly moral, and the same grammar rules were rehearsed over and over again. The English teachers droned on a great deal about "the beauties of nature," but there was little hint in their voices of the splendid imaginative qualities of the authors they read. Wordsworth's "Daffodils" was a great favorite with them. It was so utterly benign, so happily devoid of any intemperate need.

The morality issue was transformed, strangely enough, by a gifted lay teacher who made a pacifist out of me, the terror of University Avenue. Subject as we were to fairly strict discipline, we were usually merciless to the occasional interloper, who thought teaching in a Catholic girls' school might be a congenial experience. But Miss Melville had the force of character of any three nuns put together, which is force indeed. She organized history classes around debating sessions, stimulating us to think in critical terms about such issues as whether there could ever be a just war, whether it was moral to use the atom bomb or to enforce capital punishment. Under her influence I infiltrated the school paper to take up the cudgels of the Catholic left wing against my fellow Aquinites.

Miss Melville belonged to the Catholic Worker movement, dedicated to social change through the combined effort of workers and intellectuals. She introduced us to Dorothy Day and Ammon Hennessey, conscientious objectors who lived in extreme poverty serving the poor. We subscribed to their newspaper, read their articles and books, and visited their house on Christie Street. To tell the truth, I was overwhelmed by the broken and diseased men and women I met there. Christianity has a tendency to idealize poverty, make it sweet and chaste like the bodies of Carmelite nuns. Here was poverty that smelled of urine and unwashed feet—hard to relate to that Divine Plan we kept hearing about. But I idolized Miss Melville and tried to emulate her. She was a deeply serious woman with a fortunate sense of humor, who convinced many of us that our choices in life could have immense consequence.

In history class, discussion was heated and exhilarating and often kept us arguing through the corridors for the rest of the day. We rarely talked about what went on in our homes or in our inmost hearts. Our bent was theoretical and satiric and, thanks to Miss Melville, weirdly theological. She encouraged our reading of *St. Augustine's Confessions,* the *Summa Theologica,* and the *Degrees of Knowledge* by Jacques Maritain. We debated with monkish fervor the relation of good and evil, the problem of free will, the nature of God. We were comfortably in tune with twelfth-century Scholastics expostulating with one another over the distinction between essence and existence, contingent and subsistent being. We never discussed sex or fashion, never stooped to any discussion merely of men. We preferred the abstract dilemma to the personal and perpetual ones that dogged our lives.

In school competitive behavior was discouraged. Whatever its draw-backs and its implications in later life, particularly for women, the lack of competitive pressure fostered a degree of autonomy. If one were so in-clined, one worked for oneself for the pleasure of mastering the thing, a habit encouraged by the best teachers. As good St. Thomas would have it, "man's end (our end) is to know." The obverse side of this belief, the source of considerable vanity, was that by holding back, keeping things to oneself, one resisted the system. One might appear docile and obedient, but one was secretly aloof. None of my friends talked about grades, or ad-mitted to studying for exams, or to harboring any worldly ambitions. Having been to Christie Street, how could we? Most of our classmates expected to become nurses or secretaries until such time as they could swing into their true vocations as wives and mothers. The daughters of Irish, Italian, and Hispanic families were not expected to attend college. Several were actively prevented from doing so and married to escape those families soon after high school. To acquaint us further with the value of humility and obedience, certain nuns regularly lopped off ten or twenty points from our grades. They had no doubt that intellectual val-ues were subordinate to moral ones. Sisters Helena and Immaculata probably had to struggle with that proposition. Miss Melville always equated them.

At home the immigrant dream was going sour. Our apartment seemed shabby and, as much as I admired Dorothy Day, I wished we had money to brighten it up. We had, however, acquired a telephone, which seemed at first a wonderful modern advantage, starkly black and streamlined on the hall table all by itself. But with time it had the bizarre effect of increasing our estrangement. Instead of frequent visits from the family, we had telephone calls. Worst of all, hearing my father's voice over this instrument for the first time I scarcely recognized him; his accent was so thick and strange. He seemed to be talking from a different century, to be encrusted with a set of convictions I wanted now to shed. I began to feel embarrassed seeing him coming along in his shiny brown gabardine jacket and grey weathered fedora. His stories seemed less interesting. The old country really sounded old, outworn, faded in its luster. Hearing him coming home very quietly at five-thirty in the morning after working a sixteen-hour shift didn't help matters. Nor did his waiting near the bus stop, discreetly out of view, to make sure I got home safely on Saturday nights.

No doubt I was furious with him because he worked so hard and complained so little and let Mother get away with murder. Patience was a virtue that turned my stomach. Mother regularly stormed around the house, serving up thunderbolts along with the evening meal. Father would remonstrate mildly and reasonably before starting in to do the laundry—by hand.

How was I to get out of this? Or did I even contemplate escape from the developing family nightmare? The familiar form was retreat, with which we were all comfortable—except for Agnes, who was resolutely set on independence from the age of two. But retreat had been cut off; the house in Greenwood Lake was sold so that we could "be properly brought up, properly educated." Neither parent ever made that connection for us, ever blamed us directly, but there it was, too basic and unrelenting a fact to be overlooked. With it went our emotional balance, a way of nurturing ourselves.

The loss was far greater for them, of course. Now they were landless people. Come down in the world. The result was a kind of paralysis—that old Dublin affliction. Thus we were tied to the past generations, to all their years of loss and sorrow, wanting to make it up to them, even when they were inconsolable. For one who spent considerable time gazing at bridges, I had no notion of getting to the other side. No idea of progress, I suppose. Though Father had urged me to "step along, step along," I was still a dawdler, stalled at the intersection. I couldn't even imagine a final exit from the Bronx, though in the early fifties, before

Robert Moses started smashing his way through to the east, destroying neighborhoods along the route of the Cross Bronx Expressway, there were signs of decay. Our apartment house, like those of some of our friends, began to look dingy; repairs were not being made. The Major Deegan was grinding down the lovely park land by the river, and across the river in Highbridge Park the woods began to burn.

An unnatural calm settled over the block as the usual culprits came of age and went off to high school or joined a religious order. Amazing, the number of vocations hidden in those cranky interiors. Lonesome after them, I came home as late as possible from school and there hid in a book. I liked to read about merry old England or, gazing across the river, imagine living in a windy tower, furnished with the odd bit of tapestry and a lute. In time I might begin to look like Christina Rossetti or the Blessed Damosel. Forget the Lily Maid of Astolat. There was considerable pleasure in this notion of myself as hungry, threadbare, and poetic. I felt singled out for a special vocation, which would be revealed in due course and with an appropriate sign. This gave me a sense of distinction, which I craved almost as much as I craved belonging to some powerful anonymous missionary force or some sublime community.

SOUNDINGS

In my baby days I was a fashion plate. Aunts as well as parents decked me out in little frocks of velvet and taffeta, swimsuits with polka dots, hand-knit sweaters, coats with embroidered collars and matching knickers, a fur muff. As the firstborn child in America, I was a triumph. But time, alas, and other expenses and not enough income took their toll here as in everything else. By my early teens there was little in my wardrobe aside from my school uniform and various relics passed along through the family. In summer I got along with baggy jeans and sweaters, selected one size larger than necessary—though not by me—for the sake of modesty and economy. Agnes, poor soul, eventually inherited the lot. She also received in season one fluffy dress to camouflage what was regarded with old-world eyes as an unbecoming thinness.

Most of my friends were in the same predicament, so there was no cringing behind closed doors. I went about moodily, my hair cut short and frizzy, *Paradise Lost* under my arm. A pleasing disguise. When a job at Woolworth's put money in my pocket, I adopted the whimsical costume of the day—a flower at the throat, ballet slippers, a black skirt made buoyant by a crinoline and tightly cinched at the waist.

The social event of our junior year was a real prom, for which, despite the way males had been factored out of our existence, we had to have a real escort. We also had to have a snazzy dress (long hours in Woolworth's), four-inch heels, and a corsage pinned to our modest bosoms (which were inspected at the door). The great task before us then, despite all our talk about mutable and immutable essences, was to find that escort. I never broached this subject with my intellectual pals, but teamed up with a pretty Puerto Rican girl who had a tiny waist, large dark eyes, and beautiful clothes. She looked just the way I would have preferred to look. In her company, I figured, my chances would be pretty good. We all worked in teams.

There didn't seem to be any suitable males left in our parish. The most attractive were off somewhere praying and fasting, determined to be priests. We had been taught never to so much as glance at any but a Catholic boy (suppose we had a child of *mixed faith!*). So there was little choice but to scour the far corners of the Bronx, taking bus after bus across town to whatever parish, Our Lady of Perpetual Help, St. Jude's (for desperate cases), was holding a dance that weekend.

There was a curious, undeviating pattern to these dances. The girls favored maxi skirts and white lacy blouses. The boys wore jackets and ties and were expected to escort home the girl with whom they danced that fateful last dance. While the band played overtures, the boys stood hunched together—just as they had in grammar school. We girls would twirl by, doing tricky little steps in our ballerina slippers, though not too tricky lest we scare them off altogether. You could not—God forbid!—ask a boy to dance or even talk to him first without being introduced. Even eye contact was frowned upon. You might seem forward, the kind of girl who *might let a boy get away with anything*.

Being extremely nearsighted, I couldn't make eye contact anyhow. All I could do was smile foggily into space, hoping for some enchanted stranger or at least someone taller than me. (I had noticed that the short guys were the most aggressive, and they really liked to dance.) Despite the rigid codes by which we maneuvered, it was curiously romantic in those dark parish halls with a band playing the melancholy love songs of the fifties. We were a fairly innocent lot, I suppose, full of dreamy expectations of what could only be imagined as connubial bliss. Cheek to cheek, we were firmly polite. Of course we knew the priests were around somewhere keeping an eye on things and holding the fort against the guys with the black leather jackets and grease on their hair.

At long last, no doubt dazzled by the hip-swinging confidence of my Savoy (quintessentially Bronx), an appropriate young man placed himself in my path, his partner discreetly tripping off with my partner. Success! A regular date in hand. Someone to take me to Loew's Paradise on Saturday nights and feed me hot fudge sundaes in Krums. Someone—if we didn't drive each other crazy first—to take to the junior prom.

High school dating was the usual abnormal experience, colored, of course, by the habits and expectations of the time. The boys from Fordham Prep and Regis, at least the ones I managed to meet, behaved like model Christians. They came dressed as befitting a formal occasion and communicated as if by transatlantic cable. It seems to me that we all did a great deal of playacting, modeling ourselves after the demure images of the fifties: June Allyson and Jimmy Stewart, for Heaven's sake, the undisputed sweethearts of Eisenhower's America. At seventeen, wandering the pleasant groves of Pelham Bay with a boy named Jim McDermott, I received an offer of marriage like a sliver of cake on a Wedgewood platter. Was it meant for consumption? I refused as decorously as he had offered but went along to meet his parents anyhow. This was a new avenue of development. They were American parents, both of whom worked and apparently with some success; they were slim, youthful, well dressed, confident. The whole family was on a first-name basis; there was no talk of "Mom" or "Dad." Hal and Nancy had a spacious apartment, handsomely furnished. They knew about Chinese cooking and good restaurants. They even had a boat. In the middle of this civil triumvirate, I was conscious of a whole new spectrum of power. Everyone was so gracious, so well behaved, so eager to please. I was tempted to stretch out and mash a toe.

But eleven years of Catholic schooling had conditioned me not to act impulsively in public. Politeness was a great strategy. As a result, of course, there remained a gap of understanding between genders. Boys were still a separate species with whom we enjoyed certain customary rituals: the prom, the midnight ferry ride to Staten Island, the senior supper at Tavern on the Green. Such evenings were triumphs of illusion, the girls like gilded lilies, the boys white-jacketed white knights, all of us giddy with pleasure at being on the threshold of adult life. Jammed into taxis after the dance, we sped toward a sublime and sparkling Manhattan. There were no skeptics among us. Tuned to the circumference of our own charmed circle, we were all figures of romance.

My sense of belonging to a no man's land was encouraged at home as well as in school. Agnes and I were secretive. Had our parents found us out, they would have been amused, if not downright dismissive. Boys were always introduced noncommittally as "friends." Irish parents are not keen on early marriage, if indeed they are keen on marriage at all. "What's the hurry? Aren't we all fine as we are?" A gentleman caller was partially ignored—Father withdrew behind his newspaper—or else treated sardonically as physically unfortunate and politically unsound. "Though"—Mother might interject—"he has nice manners." So accustomed were we to this negative reception that if Mother took a shine to anyone (Father never did), we were immediately suspicious. Something was wrong. He was too agreeable, too "nice," dull. A husband was no guarantee of happiness, and besides there was plenty of time.

"Plenty of time." An idea that seeped in through the placenta and was well nourished. It has been difficult to dislodge. On the one hand, we were trained to be punctual; that was courtesy. On the other, there was the whole of eternity stretching amiably ahead. Such a set of beliefs did not inspire material ambition. And there was in my family a fine Irish disdain for business which, of course, none of us, except one clever, well-tailored uncle, ever understood. We hardly thought of testing out the fast track or—Heaven forbid—becoming rich! Though, now that I think of it, Mother occasionally suggested such a goal, but not with any great conviction. "Marry a rich man," she might say in humor (we assumed this was humor). It was Father who made a decisive move. Having heard my knees knocking through several singing auditions, he relinquished all hope of another Lily Pons and determined to make a teacher out of me. He took me driving through little towns in Westchester, pointing out the more attractive schools, planning things. What a comedown! From the stage to the classroom, from ermine to chalk. Surely there were more sparkling possibilities. A philosopher, an astronomer, a star gazer, certainly. Not a monitor of tests.

The trick was to ease my way out of the home nest and discover what was out there. Manhattan, alas, was foreign territory, ventured to occasionally for a film, a Gershwin concert at the Lewisohn Stadium, a stroll though Central Park. I had little sense of the awesome resources of that neighboring island, tuned as I was to a different psychic register.

Here, in the question of leaving the Bronx, as in so many things, there was little pressure from time. Indeed, with Irish parents there is much the reverse sort of pressure. A subtle, largely unconscious element was operating against me; let us call it the undertow of Irish history. It was as though I were still journeying to America. I had landed on the beach, struggled inland past the sand dunes and the swamp grass, but could not locate the way through to the interior. Unlike many children of immigrants, I was ambivalent about leaving home, where I was protected, doted upon, but made to feel guilty about the very idea of abandoning that older generation. Even a job away from home at a summer camp constituted "abandonment." As a result I developed a conflicted heart, a longing for wide open spaces, and a compulsion to dig in and rebuild that lost home under Ben Bulben.

During my seventeenth summer, I began to stretch my limited horizons. Having worked my way up the merchandise ladder, I landed a job in Cushman's Bakery on Fordham Road. Ah, where are the cakes of yesteryear? Those tempting trays of charlotte russe topped with real cream; orange, lemon, and mocha layer cakes brushed with coconut, sprinkled with hazelnuts; brownies, apple tarts, and peerless lemon meringue pie? Cushman's desserts were old favorites, and they could be had without securing a bank loan.

Most mornings it was my shop. I was responsible for the sales and the inventory. I was also entitled to damaged goods. But I was too pleased with having both hands on the tiller to dip them into the strudel. After a brisk few hours serving up blue-wrapped parcels of cake, as partial to my wares as if I had baked them, I was free. Indeed I could have gone anywhere at all, provided I was home exactly on time and there did exactly what was expected of me. The tacit agreement was that I would always be somewhere inside the Bronx.

Bathing suit and towel under my arm, I usually headed for Orchard Beach. Sometimes I went with Agnes or friends, sometimes alone, even enjoying the bus ride, hot and dusty at first and then cool and delicious as we sped toward Pelham Bay with its lovely conjunction, along a nine-mile coastline, of wooded parkland and sea. When I was licensed to drive, I visited the fishing wharves on City Island, originally Great Minnefords Island, whose eighteenth-century inhabitants plotted independence from New York. More often I meandered north along the shore road to the solitary stretches of Glen Island. On summer evenings the famous fading casino, its high deck overlooking the water, was a favorite place for dancing and listening to the mellow sound of Glenn Miller.

On summer afternoons I loved to be at the beach, good old Orchard Beach with its crescent of white sand fringed with striped umbrellas, its boardwalk which led away from a central plaza gay with marigolds, petunias, and bright pennants. The water was clear and mild; tiny fish nipped at your ankles if you waited too long at the shallow edge. I used to swim lazily from one end of the beach to the other, enjoying the sensation of being far out beyond the other swimmers. I nurtured the illusion that I could continue effortlessly on up the eastern seaboard out of reach of the whistle-blowers on the shore. When the beach was crowded, I would dive off the pier at the northern tip where the water was colder and rougher. Here there were sharp rocks and few illusions.

With more and more concrete being poured into Highbridge and the parks converted into "projects," there was still many a pleasant retreat in the Bronx. Orchard Beach and Pelham Bay, where the pioneering Anne Hutchinson once lived and where in 1776 John Glover held off the British army, were favored in summer. Van Cortlandt Park, where George Washington camped in 1781, was memorable for ice skating on its frozen lake in winter and every kind of sport all year round. There was Bronx Park, favored more for its collection of crocodiles and boa constrictors than for its rare hybrid plants. There were innumerable and delightful small parks. Every neighborhood had one, some with fine distinctive features, like the Lorelei Fountain in Joyce Kilmer Park or the splendid chestnut trees in Franz Sigel Park on the Grand Concourse. The great parks are still there, of course, though their vast expanse—more than four thousand acres—has been whittled down, neglected, crisscrossed by highways.

Growing up, I was aware of the track of the Revolutionary War through the Bronx, but it is only recently that I've become interested in the particulars of that history and in topographical details that have vanished along with actual structures, such as the forts that once protected the east shore of the Harlem River from University Heights to Kingsbridge Road. Part of the appeal of my old neighborhood was that "backward look" that the Irish love. Not knowing the particulars as a child, I could imagine a royal hand had placed that Gothic stone tower, two hundred feet high, on my horizon. Not knowing about the Hessians landing in Highbridge Park to storm Fort Washington, I could people it with dwarfs.

But old maps and prints suggest stories that are more curious than any I dreamed up. Nineteenth-century painters looked at the High Bridge with romantic eyes, softening the rugged landscape, placing sailboats on the river, peopling the foreground with couples in elegant clothes. A photograph of Ogden Avenue from the same era represents a crude frame house fronted by a dirt yard in which there are two plainly dressed women and a number of chickens. These were early inhabitants of Highbridge, originally Highbridgeville, which was settled mainly by Irish laborers who built the Croton water system in the 1840s. Highbridge itself had no water or gas or fire and police protection, but there was a school.

Early maps reveal a different irony. Along the eastern side of Mullaly Park, beneath the path of the Jerome Avenue El, there used to be large creek running into the Harlem River near Devoe's Point, an earlier name for the area. It was called Cromwell's Creek after a miller descended from a brother of Oliver Cromwell, who was remembered bitterly more than three centuries later for walling up the Irish in their churches and burning them alive. There is the name marking the old border of Highbridge.

In the 1940s and early 1950s, the landscape invited reflection. One was conscious of fragments of history, glimpses of what had not altogether passed away. There was still a sense of continuity with an older way of life evident in the small frame houses with their gardens, the lamplights, cobbled streets, and open space. It was not difficult to think even farther back in time and imagine the Bronx, like upper Manhattan, as a forest inhabited by wolves and great herds of elk and deer. Highbridge was part of a tract of land called Keskeskech by its original inhabitants. A 1927 history of the area strikes an elegiac tone: "In its wild state it must have presented sylvan scenes of surpassing beauty. Today much of that beauty is retained and there are points of vantage where the vistas of hill and stream are worth coming from afar to see." One of the earliest deeds of land purchased from the native inhabitants concedes to the Dutch owners in 1664 the right "quietly to possess . . . the meadows, uplands and trees and whatsoever else besides be upon ye said parcel of land," stating further that "their cattle may range in the Wood so Farre as they please."* A pastoral note, with a certain Irish resonance, carrying the familiar memory of displacement and loss.

NO CELESTIAL SIGNPOST

The Bronx was a state of mind, insular and familiar. I was in no hurry to move on.

Much of my last year at Aquinas High School was spent at a local hangout with friends swilling coke and plotting our brilliant careers. We were full of plans, "dream plans," you might say, because they were so little compromised by actual information. We were the perfect products of an education that emphasized the historical and theoretical. No one was inclined to knock on corporate doors in Manhattan, although we liked to think of ourselves as chic executive types traveling the high road from Paris to Hong Kong. Our goal was to take in as much of the *WORLD*, writ in large radiant letters, as possible. Peering out foggily from our Victorian demesne, that is what we thought we wanted.

Which professions might enable us to achieve this ambition—the means to a lofty end—was not clear either. The law had a fine, leather-bound, scholarly appeal, and there were years of preparation before one actually had to face a client. None of us, of course, knew any lawyers or any professional women for that matter (forget about teachers). Hence the drift and the inclination to extend the present by settling down on another congenial plateau where we could continue to explore mutable and immutable essences. No one mentioned success. No one mentioned money. There were plenty of dawdlers in the Bronx.

* Wells, James L., et al. *The Bronx and Its People,* 4 vols. New York: Lewis Historical Publications (1927, 312–16).

What was emphatically agreed upon was that marriage should be avoided as long as possible. The morning we graduated from Aquinas, a classmate who had dropped out to marry was giving birth. We thought of her with pity. Perhaps we had grown too accustomed to the company of women, but it seemed then that marriage with its attendant swarm of children would put an end to our bright dreams, finish us off just as it had our mothers. At that age, with all our illusions about independence of mind, no one renounced the Church position on birth control. There seemed to be only two alternatives: One either submitted to the divine scheme or one evaded it entirely. Evasion was a skill we thought we had mastered.

With these friends, I went on amiable, unofficial excursions to local colleges, like Fordham and Mount St. Vincent, in scenic locations. We sat in on philosophy classes, had tea with the dean—fakers that we were—put ourselves forward as aspiring candidates. None of us could afford these schools nor, God help us, did we think of practical schemes for gaining entrance. We had all applied to Hunter College, the democratic choice, and one which took determination because the nuns shredded our applications until we found them out. In the meantime there were hours of blithe conversation and the pleasure of browsing in scholarly pastures, but little resolution. It was as though (a recurring conceit) I were waiting around in the vestibule of fate for some powerful summons.

And sure enough it came. A visitor appeared from a women's college in Maryland, offering scholarships and new horizons. Oh! The comedy of the thing. I thought the world was my oyster.

I prepared for college with something of the inspired resolve of early Irish monks sailing into the Atlantic without so much as a sextant or a navigational chart. I took no heed of catalogs or any useful description of the place or the student body or the course of study that was offered. I was the first of our family to enter college, indeed to enter high school, so college took on the trappings of an archetypal quest. I was so full of vapory notions I might have been headed for the salmon-colored towers of Salamanca and not a sleepy little farming town in Maryland. It did not occur to me in my innocence that one institution of higher learning might differ substantially from another. I tended to fit reality to an ideal, if indeed I noticed the "reality" at all. But that's not quite accurate: I noticed it all right but didn't allow it to interfere with the cherished dream.

That summer before college had a kind of purgatorial splendor. It was a summer of abstinence, with not a shred of pleasure, which of course is pleasure for those with ascetic inclinations. Every penny had to be saved. With Patsy Rourke, a friend on a similar transcendental mission, I worked as a typist in one of the larger corporate beehives downtown. Poor drones, we typed wearily seven hours a day for fifty dollars a week, our fingers numb, our eyes blurry. Manhattan was then, and no doubt remains, predominantly powered by males, aggressive, fierce, and condescending. Working there as a student, I was regarded as one more morsel to be swallowed up. My combative instincts had been dulled by years of parochial schooling. I was polite to monsters. Unable to meet them on their own terms, I countered with secret contempt, withdrawn and impregnable behind my Remington Rand. At lunchtime Patsy and I took our sandwiches and two teabags to Horn and Hardart, helped ourselves to hot water, and settled down to scholarly discourse. Thus we preserved our integrity in the marketplace.

At home there were unmistakable signs of crisis. Heavy silences, tears. An Irish mother in the true primordial mold does not readily relinquish her offspring. She views any change with alarm, and none more so than the prospect of their leaving home—for any reason. Classes were well under way before she capitulated and only on the condition that the entire family escort me there to look the place over—just to be sure it was safe. This venture had all the earmarks of an evacuation in wartime, except that it was accomplished at our customary leisurely pace. Father always preferred the back roads to the direct connection studded with tollbooths. Perhaps he couldn't resist the opportunity of seeing more of the country, and he never trusted maps. It took us two days to locate Maryland.

Here my life took a turn that was—to say the least—ironic. I was prepared mentally to sit at the footstool of Abelard, stylus in hand, and in a sense that was precisely where I found myself. St. Joseph's College was full of contradictions, both pleasant and maddening, that had little to do with modern times. The first thing that impressed me and soothed my aboriginal cravings was the landscape: a line of low hills, a wilderness on the horizon; in the foreground, an immense lawn bordered by sycamore trees; and beyond that patches of farmland with small herds of cattle. The college was a congenial red-brick cluster, housing a few excellent lay instructors, single-minded, unworldly, and underpaid. My mentor was the dean of students, very tall and elegant in her sweeping full skirts and the white-winged headdress of a French order of nuns. She was an ethereal presence who loaned me books and encouraged my late night Bunsen-burning propensities. The students were fairly diverse in background, many of them intellectually serious and well read. There were several daughters of army officers as well as unreconstructed Southerners with languorous voices and a harsh view of Yankees. There were also girls from wealthy Latin American families, homesick and very pious. The rest came from Boston, Washington, and other eastern cities. Thus I got a taste of a more varied cultural world.

On campus, however, we lived in a kind of time warp because of the pervasive presence of the nuns, who taught many of the classes, and whose mother house adjoined the academic buildings. There was a medieval flavor about the place after all. Our lives were ordered with great strictness: breakfast at eight, classes at nine, lunch at noon, town from three to five, dinner at six, choir at seven, back to the dorm by eight-thirty on weeknights. We signed in and out under the scrutiny of a housemother and could travel legally only within a discreet radius of the college without special permission. Nothing was left to chance or individual whim. There were regulations governing everything from dress to attendance in chapel, and it took very few violations to find oneself confined to campus for a week at a stretch. We were allowed to meet gentlemen callers—a major concession—but only during certain hours in highly visible, usually well-chaperoned locations. The system was enforced by student monitors, who were both incorruptible and equipped with excellent eyesight.

St. Joseph's was that most Catholic of institutions: a retreat for study and contemplation. How unerringly I made my way there! Not for me the fleshpots of Greenwich Village or the blandishments of the avant-garde. I had found the North American equivalent of the monastic settlement at Glendalough in County Wicklow. Had I been able to locate St. Kevin's Kitchen, I'd have climbed right in. Me and Pangur Ban, the scholar and her cat.

There can be few students more serious than I was then, or more humorless. So determined was I to make up for lost time, for all those daydreaming, misspent hours, I took on as large and varied a course load as

St. Joseph's allowed, organizing my efforts according to a new sense of hierarchy. Literature now seemed frivolous, philosophy was hopelessly skewed; it was science that drew me, like Sisyphus to his rock, the moth to the flame. Here was a body of quantifiable fact, an ostensibly objective, pristine, and beautifully articulated system that resisted the buttery grasp of pious fingers. I knew every formula in my chemistry text. Every single one. Molecular structure was irresistible. Had I stayed longer, I would probably have had to be scraped from the lab chair and carried off to an asylum. The place encouraged unnatural ambitions in those with a certain cast of mind, like medieval scribes copying out by hand—those elegant hands—the entire store of learning.

In my sophomore year a portion of our class, mainly those on scholarship (hence our resentment), was moved while the dorms were being renovated. All our belongings—Bermuda shorts, white buckskin shoes, the quaint paraphernalia of the fifties—were bundled summarily under the nunnery roof. My new roommate, Jeanne Cramer, was an aristocratic spirit, enamored of Russian music and Latin ritual, who never allowed herself to be disturbed one jot by the incipient craziness of the place.

In the room next door was a very beautiful and diabolical nun, the housemother, who seemed to know more about us, and particularly about the men in our lives, than we could account for. She glided through the corridors on invisible feet, smiling a Mona Lisa smile. Occasionally, she would pin us with a direct, pertinent question, mischief written on her perfectly chiseled features, judgment in her violet eyes. Could she hear us through the walls? We wondered about her all alone at night in that narrow room, the contents of which were always concealed. Why had such a gorgeous creature chosen such a life?

Much as it disturbed me, the place had an otherworldly charm as had the Carmelite convent on University Avenue. One was always conscious of the nuns in their winged headdresses. One would hear them getting up at five o'clock, hear them rustling through the upper stories much of the day, fervid and chaste. But the Carmelites had remained in their cloister, a delicate presence, a spiritual resource. These nuns were determined to stamp us with the values of their lives. They held up a standard of womanliness, which I confess appealed to me—the lace curtain syndrome—as it satisfied a longing for graciousness and style. But it was better than that.

Behind the prettiness was a sincerity and intelligence. One was not barred for lack of funds.

So what was the problem, apart from the matter of surveillance, of course? Perhaps it was best reflected in a task that both pleased and appalled me deeply. In the absence of males, we had the responsibility of offering the response to the college chaplain during daily Mass. Jeanne and I took our turn together, rising at dawn and slipping down quietly to the chapel, lacy white veils on our bowed heads, Latin missals in our hands. We were not permitted on the altar but took our places kneeling on a pretty little prie-dieu just outside the sanctuary. The configuration was clear, and it rankled in my soul—my Bronx Irish soul, no doubt. Despite the thrust of my religious upbringing or, paradoxically, because of it, I expected to be treated like everyone else, men included.

I began staying away from chapel, breaking the innumerable rules. Resistance cheers me up, forestalls the family curse of melancholy. After all, the family for all their pride about sticking to the high moral ground were not sticklers for rules. Once you fought your way across the threshold of adulthood—and there was certainly a fight—you were expected to work things out for yourself, "stand on your own two feet," as they would say.

I decided to leave at the end of the term. Reluctant though I was to return to the gusty enclosure of family life, it was better than being shackled in Emmitsburg. Whatever doubts I had were dispelled by an unexpected confrontation that gave me a startling view of the warty underbelly of convent life.

A crowd of us had just returned from a midterm break in Washington, D.C., which included a full-scale dress ball in the Southern fashion: waltzing by candlelight, gardenias, swirls of organdy and lace, delicious down to the last giddy detail. We were summoned before the college president, normally a mild sort of woman, and thrashed for two hours. What had gone on after the ball was over at the Shoreham Hotel? Despite the platoon of chaperones? Despite the permission of parents and the orthodoxy of all living arrangements? She was rancorous with suspicion. No one got supper. No one confessed.

Sister Concepta kept me after letting the rest go, thinking I was obliged, as her assistant and one who received tuition free of charge, to be her informant. She stated as much, wilting my pride, and we went through the whole thing again. It finally occurred to me that she wanted to be told something intimate and terrible. As she came toward me from behind her desk, her face was grey-white and soggy, the teeth exposed, the corners of her mouth puckered and cruel. She was sure we had done something. What was it? When I backed away, she persisted, pressing closer, her breath sour, the wimple wrinkling on her forehead. I should tell her everything. Indeed.

The next day she was all smiles. Nothing more was said about the Washington trip, but her secretary informed me that henceforth I would be working in the library, the bowels of the library, then in the eye-wrecking process of shifting to the Library of Congress classification system. The consequences didn't stop there, but the details scarcely matter. I was winnowed out from the ranks of the faithful, the chaff from the wheat. I lost my little perks, my privileged little spot in the sun. The miserable truth is I was as faithful as she could have wished.

In her cunning way, she had sensed the turmoil I thought so well concealed by my scholarly decorum. There was a sensual wind blowing through that lovely countryside; indeed, it blew around Washington. That spring the scent of honeysuckle was everywhere, and the lush wisteria vine snaked its way along the border of our little enclave. But I felt locked out, disbarred, as though the gates of Eden had closed against me. Emotions struck with a force that was confusing, try as I did to consign them to categories along with the nine beatitudes and the seven deadly sins. Day-to-day living at the college was charged with tension. Chastity was the norm, revered by the church and practiced devoutly by the nuns with whom we were cloistered. But then, the nuns did not have to contend with a real—if Catholic—male driving along the foggy winding roads of a Maryland night. There was always a chaperone either in the car up ahead or following somewhere close behind. But fog is fog. Never have I felt so much like Eve itching to get my hands on that apple.

I didn't think of the loss of virginity as the loss of "a priceless jewel," as some priests would have it. I thought the results would be more concrete, like a one-way ticket to Hell. Or was it to Kubla Khan? I couldn't determine. In my experience the erotic was not so much suppressed as charged with abnormal tension by the threat of retribution. Dante's sinful lovers swim eternally in a bath of fire. Not the worst possibility in his Inferno.

Yet I held back, morbidly romantic and Christian. If I was going to be damned, I wanted to be damned with the right partner. The tweedy, pipe-smoking Philadelphian with whom I was driving so precariously was really too lacking in temperament for my taste, too orthodox, too "nice." Or so I reasoned, wrapping myself in chains of hydrocarbons and breaking off the match. Nor was I consistent, a quality I used to admire. The minute he took up with another girl, I set my lures to win him back and then broke it all up again.

Fortunately the body has a way of striking a balance when one is about to slide over a precipice, moral or psychic. After I had catalogued innumerable books, fuming away, bitter and miserable underground, my eyesight gave out. One eye was patched, and I was warned not to read anything for the rest of the semester. So much for crystalline structures, final exams, and the perfect index. There was nothing to do but stretch out under the sycamore trees and relax.

I went back to the Bronx, regretful, missing friends and my smelly corner of the lab, thoroughly angry and disillusioned. It was hard to disconnect myself from that pleasant, punishing place in which I had invested so much aspiration and energy. It was hard to forget that astonishing, crazy nun. I brooded over it for years. Women in the fifties moved timidly. And I was an emotional bag lady, hauling alone a fabulous collection of West of Ireland, Catholic, immigrant, working-class, humanist assumptions.

Finally enrolled at Hunter College, I was happy in the total anonymity of the place. Aside from Agnes, who was also matriculating, I knew no one; no one knew me or cared one jot about my moral development. Encouraged by excellent professors, I turned back to the study of literature: Shakespeare, Yeats, Austen, the Romantic poets, all my old loves. I went along at an easier rhythm, found my way without the usual celestial signposts. Eventually, I met gay students and black students and veterans of the Korean War. In philosophy I became friendly with a young woman who was divorced. Agnes, the realist, was taking me in hand. She figured I had been circling in Ptolemy's universe long enough.

Maureen and her mother, Agnes Waters. Franz Sigel Park.
Courtesy of the author.

MYTHOLOGIES

The Irish imagination—like the Jewish imagination—has been said to compensate for material and emotional loss. In the sixteenth and seventeenth centuries, when monasteries were sacked, priests and poets outlawed, land and cattle confiscated, the Irish held on to their stories. Religious and cultural traditions have encouraged an otherworldly consciousness in which the eternal perpetually outweighs the experience of time. What is to come, what can only be imagined, is the higher order, what the Irish term "the fifth province," a supernatural realm bordering the other four.

When I was growing up, everything of importance was endowed with some transcendent meaning, giving me a sense of inner strength, coherence, and purpose. I seldom saw the tree in front of me on its own terms; it was usually blooming in this otherworldly perspective. This tendency has distinct advantages in times of scarcity and frost.

Working the garden here in New Paltz, I am well aware of the limitations imposed by the extremes of climate and poor soil. My flowers bloom fitfully, shrubs are often stunted, or when they flourish, the deer consume them. They get all the hybrid lilies. Working on hands and knees during the heat of the summer, fertilizing, loosening the hard-packed soil near the roots, I feel the tentativeness of this garden, but with my dreaming eye I visualize the blossoming hills of the Butchart Gardens, which I have visited in British Columbia. My scraggly roses are infused with gardens of the mind.

The Heathcliff syndrome is an unfortunate effect of this mythologizing tendency. In my case it was exacerbated by life in the cloister—walled in by one set of ideas, isolated by gender, culture, religion; as a result given to daydreams. To see oneself as a character in a romance, rather than as a person with real needs, is a habit best shed with adolescence. In many ways during my college years I had not outgrown the child sleighing in the park, depending on a powerful male to carry her to that dazzling tree. Little I had learned in the Catholic schools I attended encouraged a woman to be independent or adventurous. Among my friends there was only one true individualist, Jeanne Cramer, who traveled alone through Europe on a tiny budget the summer after I was married. The most daring thing I had ever done was to leave St. Joseph's for Hunter College, a potential escape route, but I was too accustomed to the cloister to realize it at the time. Never mind Europe, I still hadn't located Manhattan.

But does this explain why I married an impossible man, an intelligent, dynamic, but ultimately brutal man? As a friend once pointed out, most Irish Catholic girls in similar circumstance didn't make such a choice.

Few are afflicted by the Heathcliff syndrome. It takes an overheated, naïve imagination as well as a rebellious wrinkle in the family genes. What is more appealing to a compulsively virtuous girl than an unconventional man of whom everyone disapproves? In female terms the obverse equivalent of Stephen Dedalus's "wild angel" is the demon lover, who releases you from one form of bondage but compels you to another.

He settled beside me in French class, which I was taking in the expectation of exotic pleasures to come. How droll. How effectively I always managed to box myself in. He leaned toward me, immediately fogging my judgment, an arrogant, good-looking man who had already dumped the shibboleths of his own immigrating forebears. Jason certainly wasn't tied to his mother's apron strings. He wasn't Irish. Nor was he keen on Jesus. He was unlike anyone else I had ever met, and he quickly determined to marry me. Indeed I was overwhelmed by that determination. A man accustomed to getting his way, he could be charming, considerate, passionate in pursuing whatever he wanted, and he wanted a great deal. The scale of his ambitions excited me, entangled as I was in those Bronx roots. In four months we were married. Given my abnormal dearth of experience and peculiar mind-set, it couldn't have happened in any other way.

From a certain point of view, ours was a comical courtship. All those dikes created by masses, novenas, rosaries, the exhortations of nuns and priests, the sermons on Hell—those dikes crumbled fast. I spent considerable time wringing my hands and moping around the apartment. I dropped out of French class. My digestive system went into spasm, leaving me weirdly thin and morose. Agnes figured I was losing my mind and rightly suspected the cause. I denied everything.

When the truth came out, the whole family reacted against him. Mother immediately seized the high ground: "If you have to get married, why can't it be one of your own kind?" Agnes kept her teeth civilly embedded in her tongue so as not to laugh out loud. My usually mild-mannered father took Jason by the collar, walked him out of the kitchen, down the long hall, and out the front door of our apartment, where he offered to fling Jason—all six feet of him—down the stairs. "Fine weather be after him!" Jason had made the strategic error of interrupting our St. Patrick's Day festivities with a formal declaration of his intentions. Deluded soul, he thought my father would appreciate his speaking up like that, man to man. My father saw him as making improper advances toward *His Daughter, the Student*: "There will be plenty of time for that sort of thing a few years down the line."

For once I resisted all of them.

So we were married on a warm day in the week following my graduation from Hunter. Everything that could go wrong did go wrong (Murphy's Law). Because of a mix-up about cars, the wedding was delayed for an hour. The temperature soared above ninety degrees while the bride wilted at home and the guests wilted at church, one of the groomsmen fainting at the altar. During the reception the families on both sides avoided each other, most notably the parents. The cake was soggy. No one understood the toast offered by the best man. Yet afterwards, when the bride and groom offered a spirited rendition of their favorite song from *Oklahoma!*—"Oh! What a Beautiful Morning"—everyone applauded.

No, it wasn't love of adventure or a promising career, but an unfortunate marriage that propelled me from the Bronx. Although I didn't admit it at the time, I married hastily in part to escape problems at home. How well I succeeded! When disapproving Irish parents let go, there's a remarkable snap that sends you, as it were, catapulting through intergalactic space, so stony cold is the gulf that stretches between you. It's then that you finally have to grow up and locate America. It's then you realize what you've done to yourself.

At first I was surprised by the bouts of heavy drinking, the broken promises, the odd streak of paranoia. I was slow to understand that at rock bottom Jason didn't believe in much. Success made him cynical. Colleagues, friends, his two sons became so many objects to manipulate; their personal response was of much less interest than the business strategy of the moment. He distorted facts so readily, charmed clients so easily that, with time and the growing haze of alcoholism, his sense of reality was permanently confused. Not that it stopped him professionally, although his career followed a cyclical pattern of ups and downs, periods of feverish financial speculation, followed by collapse and then a cycle of recovery.

The marriage lasted seven years, including periods of separation and reconciliation. Then I fled my husband impulsively and desperately in a scene, not out of *Wuthering Heights* but out of *Peyton Place*. I had the two children, one suitcase, and the two thousand dollars Jason had left on the dresser before passing out over the martini pitcher. In the years since, he has married other women, fathered other children, and left them all behind. He lived for a time in the Caribbean, operated a gambling casino, edited a magazine, and sold vacuum cleaners. More recently he emerged in khaki cords, his hair cropped short, hinting at secret intelligence exploits in the Persian Gulf.

The bitterness is deep and lasting. It wells up in the throat, but there is nothing to do but spit it out and go on to other things.

Motherhood has its mythology, too, a fact well documented in modern psychology. As a young mother I was filled with customary exhilaration and dread: delighting in those first words, the first steps, that first Christmas; afraid of doing something harmful or something wrong. Giving him a bath, I was terrified of dropping my firstborn son on the kitchen floor. I had no experience of looking after tiny children whatsoever. The most important object I had ever picked up was, naturally, a book. At that very moment Dr. Spock was propped open while my good-natured mother-in-law was standing by—just in case.

Usually I was alone with the children as my husband's working hours increasingly merged with the late night bar scene. So, apart from corporate performances, my life tended to revolve around them. I read them *The Wind in the Willows* and Dr. Seuss; saw them through the measles, chicken pox, et al.; took them to the circus and *The Nutcracker*; organized birthday parties for dozens of little tots. I was often exhausted and lonely, but the boys were sturdy and intelligent and sweet, although rarely so in the middle of the night.

Left alone so much together, mother and child grow more intensely dependent on one another, and their feelings in time may curdle with resentment. In the absence of a father, Huck Finn comes of age by lighting out for the territory, leaving the women behind. Thinking of how my own mother focused her enormous energies on the family, I encouraged my sons to be self-reliant. The worst thing imaginable was that they might feel guilty or angry toward me. Sometimes I felt like the beleaguered sparrow outside my window, nudging her offspring to the edge of a branch. Willing them to fly.

I was not involved in the feminist movement of the late 1960s and the 1970s, which prompted many women of my generation to rethink their lives and throw away bras, girdles, high heels, the lot. I took a limited part in the civil rights and antiwar movements and began teaching in a college program for inner-city adults. With a child of my own on each hip, I had neither the time nor the money to demonstrate before the White House or integrate Southern lunch counters. Feminist issues seemed remote compared with the problems of earning a living, taking care of the children, and starting graduate work. Feminists had little to say about raising children anyhow. I wish I had been less shortsighted. Talking with other women, particularly those less keen on media hype, might have saved us all from the myth of the "Good Mother," allowed me to be "Good Enough," as D. W. Winnicott puts it.

While my contact with the larger America envisioned by the civil rights and antiwar movements was limited, it nonetheless allowed me to think of social issues, to take a deep breath outside the house. I understood that there were important intersections between the two spheres but didn't try to work them out. Indeed, this was a major problem until the children were grown. There was no established pattern for a woman in my situation, no support system to help her integrate the public and private spheres. Moreover, Irish pride was operating: "back to the wall, standing on your own two feet" and all that. If I had to raise these children alone, so be it. Had not my father's mother, widowed at thirty-two, raised seven of them? And what choice was there? In our family one didn't ask for help. One solved one's own problems, kept quiet, and didn't admit to deprivation or pain. It's a troubling heritage. One should be able to ask for help.

With a down payment of twelve hundred dollars, borrowed on the strength of a new teaching job, I secured a small house on Long Island. The house was gradually furnished and painted; the children were fitted out with bicycles and soccer balls. They had regular birthday parties, regular meals. They played baseball and football, joined the school band, and took karate lessons; most of the time I was there to root for them. But when I had to leave the house before they did because of our different school schedules, I felt awful. My early religious faith had eroded after the divorce. For the most part the Church's attitudes toward women seemed appalling. Nonetheless, I retained a powerful sense of Irish Catholic guilt. The Good Mother should do it all. That mythology, that totalizing instinct, is lethal. It's not the little gaps and mistakes that trouble children's lives when you love them; it's infecting them with a sense that you are in the wrong, that you are failing them.

I still see that house across a great distance as the place of expectation and promise. But Brian's death has shattered any sense of order and continuity. The details are still there, of course, etched at some subliminal level, surfacing sporadically in dreams or in broad daylight. Still a strong swimmer, in dreams I plunge into deep water over and over, trying to find him and bring him back to the surface. During the day I misplace small objects continuously, neurotically, maddeningly.

With the death of a child, one feels that one has lost an essential part of one's being, not a mere body part. I've lost a breast to cancer; it's not the same thing at all. The cut goes much deeper, into a vital inner region that I still think of as the soul. As yet I cannot grasp the pattern of Brian's life, nor its closure. Patterns to some extent are fictions, but they are comforting nonetheless. I wish I could believe in the eternal, that fifth province. I wish I had a healing mythology.

Father told his stories over and over because we loved to hear them. But it is also true, as I've come to realize, that he was struggling to clarify what had happened. There was an accumulation and a variation of detail, particularly in stories about his older brother and that nameless little child who died as he stood holding her at age eight. He was passing on to us the lesson of stoicism, of clenching your teeth so you cannot scream. My mother refused to tell, as if she were striking something dead before it could clamp her by the throat.

Maureen, six years old, and Agnes. Highbridge, 1941.
Courtesy of the author.

LOCATING AMERICA

*R*aising two children made me conscious of time; teaching drove me headlong—for better and for worse—into mainstream America. Half my life has been spent in teaching. It's doubtful that another profession could give me as much satisfaction, but I came to it by default. Before I was lured away from the Bronx, I was planning to spend the next decade in graduate school, preferably at Columbia University. A highly theoretical course of study sheltered in an ivory tower was my first choice. After that there would be fellowships and books to write. I might never have to deal with an actual student.

Marriage provided the reality principle.

I started out in 1958 as a "permanent sub" in a Queens high school, talking incessantly and teaching very little. I had thought naïvely that all those years in a classroom might translate into appropriate skills. After all, I had read the books. But it takes a lot of maneuvering on the far side of the desk to manage the dynamics of a class and engage students usefully. Armed with the usual credentials and a fine set of aspirations, I had little practical understanding of the task before me.

There was little fear of handguns, and metal detectors had yet to be installed, but classes were crowded and volatile in the public schools then as now. Colleagues joked bitterly about teaching as "crowd control." The real test of skill was no longer whether you could keep kids in the same room, but whether you could keep them on the same floor of the school. If everyone showed up for class on a particular day—unusual, of course—some had to sit on the radiator. There were only forty seats for the typical class of forty-five. My biggest problem was the senior boys, high on testosterone and low on scholarly incentive. As I took over my first class, I was warned not to turn my back on them. The trick was to wield authority up front, make it felt, make it palpable. Clearly my fresh-faced, just-out-of-pigtails look was a liability, so I adopted a geriatric disguise: dark tailored suits, knees well hidden, horn-rimmed glasses, sturdy shoes. I talked fast, gave them more notes and more tests than they bargained for, and never smiled.

That first semester three of my five classes were speech classes, for which I was not even licensed. Not having the foggiest notion of how to proceed, I began by drawing lungs and other body parts on the board to demonstrate how speech is produced. We inhaled and exhaled in a wobbly chorus. As the students had no interest whatsoever in the body parts I was illustrating, things went steadily downhill until I switched gears and began reading plays with them. Here at least I was on home territory and easily flushed out a gaggle of closet thespians.

In the late 1950s and the 1960s high school administrators worried a great deal about literature corrupting innocent teenage minds. This was a big issue at faculty meetings, where we drew up lists of books that were "safe," that is, they contained no profanity and no references to sex. Imagine where that leaves you. The resulting curriculum was far more sanitized than that of Catholic schools. *The Catcher in the Rye* was the test case, banned indefinitely or else locked in the library basement with *The Decameron.* The consequences for average or honor classes were not altogether dire as they still had Shakespeare, George Eliot, and Charles Dickens. The so-called C track, the slow learners, visibly suffered. Mostly male, many of them big, older-than-average guys, they not only had to read but to carry around for all to see such meek texts as *A Lantern in Her Hand,* by Bess Alrich.

As a sub, I managed to evade the nets of censorship by bringing the students books of my own such as *Black Boy* and *Native Son* by Richard Wright. At least the subject of race relations was real to them. Consequently I acquired a reputation for "handling" difficult kids, that is, slow learners, mainly because no problems developed while I was in charge. No one knew about my secret weapon. None of the kids ever snitched, and—their highest mark of approval—my car tires were never slashed.

I received official recognition when the principal came in to observe me. The kids, several of whom had been placed on probation by the courts, assumed he was there to check up on them. Instead of slouching in their desks, they sat with spines rigid in attention. They vied with one another to answer questions, raised their scruffy hands politely, noted down every syllable I uttered. Had I choreographed the whole thing, it couldn't have turned out better.

So there I was, poised to graduate from permanent sub to a tenure-bearing position when what might have been expected by a practicing Catholic occurred. I became pregnant. When I passed the magic marker of three months, I informed this principal, so amiable, so favorably impressed with my holding skills. Although I wasn't planning to leave until the end of the term, I thought he would need time to interview candidates for my job. A colossal mistake: I was fired on the spot, the principal grimly assuring me he had no other choice "in such a case." Was he secretly reading *The Scarlet Letter*? I was to hand in my keys and attendance records—those inimitable Delaney cards—immediately; someone else would meet my remaining classes that day. Forty-five minutes later I was out on the street, clutching a paper bag stuffed with the contents of my desk. So, Lee, my firstborn, excellent scholar, that's how your mom got expelled from school.

I didn't return to teaching until after my divorce and move to Long Island, and after the children had started school themselves. I began teaching English at Massapequa High School. It was a mad scramble. There was an agonizing gap between the children's schedule and mine, usually no more than a half hour in the morning and another half hour in the afternoon. But the logistics of securing a sitter and getting them ready were stomach-curdling. There was no time for wiping up the spilled milk, so to speak. No time for the extra little reassurances a child needs, no time for an extra piece of toast. Everything had to be done right on the first try, or it didn't get done, and everything had to be done rapidly. Try propelling two squirmy boys into snowsuits, boots, and mittens in eight minutes flat. A sudden illness could be calamitous. The single parent needs an extended family and—if not an entire village—reliable day care she can afford.

In these circumstance I didn't think much about my brilliant career. I focused on the mechanics of getting to class and somehow getting through the day without disgracing myself. My schedule included five classes and one supervisory period; there were forty-seven minutes for lunch and forty-seven minutes for "prep." Most of the prep, drawing up lesson plans and grading papers and exams, was done each evening after the boys were in bed or had settled down with a game or a book. Let me tell you, it takes a great deal of energy and night work to keep five classes going five days a week with 160 students.

Adding to the pressure was the fact that working mothers were frequently stigmatized as "unreliable." The morning I was reprimanded for being ten minutes late, I did not mention that the children were ill; putting the blame on the Long Island Railroad was more acceptable. High school principals had the kind of fixation on the clock that one would expect under the old factory piecework system. Class "modules" were scheduled for abnormal time periods, usually forty-seven minutes each, at the end of which a bell rang, and we all scampered—there was three minutes scampering time—to the next module. It did not matter what was happening at the moment that bell rang. Everyone grabbed her books and bolted for the door. Of course, one learned to teach with an eye on the clock, but that meant tight control over the natural rhythm of class discussion. I sometimes felt I was forcing kids to jump through a series of little hoops, and they all had to jump together. There was no time for the one who held back to consider his footing. Thus the rhythm at school was uncomfortably similar to that at home.

Anxiety about my job didn't prevent me from joining a newly formed teachers' union and picketing for better working conditions and decent salaries. As I've mentioned, resistance cheers me up. I may have had years of Catholic training in patience and endurance, but the Irish rebels in the family had left their imprint, too.

Maintaining such a pace meant there was little time for brooding over my emotional needs and disappointments, little time for friendship or looking around for a good man. Indeed, I didn't find one for ten years. Being situated in the suburbs didn't help matters. What got me through, I suppose, was a basic optimism fueled by modes of thinking acquired early in life. I was sure we would manage; my confidence was returning after years of shame and failure. I was convinced that I could go on catching those fast balls, that I wouldn't be struck in the face or struck out. The children were healthy and high spirited; in the midst of the daily whirl, a treasure to hold on to, to give me balance. I certainly worried about them, but they seemed reasonably happy despite the divorce and its aftermath: infrequent, emotionally charged visits from their father. Other less obvious pressures were affecting us, too, in ways I didn't fully recognize at the time.

That cherished home with its willows and rosebushes, its lilac trees and tomato patch, sprouted its share of weeds. Situated close to my school, so I could quickly respond in an emergency, it was a lonely spot for a single woman. My social contacts were limited to colleagues seen between classes or on the picket line. Worse yet, in Seaview a divorced woman or a single parent was an anomaly. Each house on our block seemed to contain two parents, two kids, two television sets, and one dog. As a result, the boys became self-conscious and vulnerable. Wanting to protect them from drugs and violence in Manhattan (an irony in itself), I brought them to a middle-class suburb, where those who were judged "different"—even the few Jewish kids—had a hard time of it. Unconsciously, I was repeating the patterns of the Bronx, trying to cloister them as well. In a more open world we would all have fared better.

But I didn't understand that then, even though professional commitments were to draw me toward the city through a job at Queens College. Young adults from ghetto areas were being prepared for matriculation there through immersion courses in English, math, history, and art, supported by a team of counselors and tutors. That was 1967, one year before open admissions at the City University of New York, the largest public university in the country, comprising twenty-one institutions. Queens is academically outstanding among the senior colleges. When I accepted the job, I was told it would probably last no more than two or three years. The plan was to hire more minority teachers and eventually to hire our own students to take our places. Not knowing what I would do afterwards, I decided to take the risk to get away from high school bureaucracy. Perhaps, more fundamentally, I had not forgotten that poverty prevented my parents from going to high school. An experimental, open-ended program intended to overcome discrimination had strong appeal.

Despite what happened later, working in this program made me feel that teaching was the right choice. Our faculty and staff were mainly young and altruistic, classes were small, and there was time to talk with students afterwards. We had to find out fast what would work, what they needed most to know, so we asked for and got plenty of direct feedback, which was how I finally learned to teach. There was immense enthusiasm all around me because so much was riding on this program. It was our students' chance for a college degree, something they had scarcely thought about before. These were internal refugees. Some had been in prison, including a fabled cat burglar from Brooklyn. All came from poor or unsettled homes; many had children of their own. We took them to the theater and to the Schomburg Library in Harlem, loaded them down with books—Shakespeare, Hemingway, Freud, James Baldwin—a feast of books.

Our classrooms were improvised spaces in and around the college. Sometimes we sat on packing cases in basement housing. I liked the informality and the innovation, and liked going to class in jeans and sneakers. Having escaped the high school routine, I worked eagerly on a new curriculum and helped to organize the day-to-day functioning of the program. The students were much more demanding than high school kids because they were older and more experienced, and that experience—some of it horrifying like that of one young woman whose mother had slashed her face with a razor and who later transferred to Yale—became a resource for writing. I was learning how to tap something valuable and real, learning to respond, to guide their response, to master it. Their willingness to say what was on their minds, instead of fencing with me or merely being polite, encouraged a corresponding directness in me.

We got to know our students fairly well, showing them how to take notes, how to prepare for exams, how to survive in college. If these first ones succeeded, approximately five hundred of them, more would follow. We were all generally fired up by the political climate of the sixties, the eagerness for social change, the confidence that it could be accomplished despite the growing disaster in Vietnam. I felt at long last I was making my way inland past the swamp grass and locating America.

Buoyed by this experience, I decided that I'd like to teach on the college level. Following the path that many women with families choose, I began working toward an doctorate in education at Columbia, "majoring"—as the common joke has it—in Thursday nights, the only time I could spare for classes in Manhattan. As a result, although I squeezed in as many literature courses as possible, graduate study was not the intellectual feast I had anticipated in the Bronx. It was spiced up hamburger swallowed on the run, a pragmatic choice that would enable me to direct a writing program, although that's not the way things turned out.

Juggling work and school and children does teach the single parent to organize by doing five or six things at once. One learns efficiency at the cost of deeply nurtured habits and predilections. One may simply be caught in a double bind. My dissertation on William Faulkner was written in two-hour stretches in the library in the course of a year. It raised pertinent questions about Faulkner's idea of women, but it didn't sparkle. At the finish, I had to climb over the prone bodies of antiwar protesters at Columbia to give the thing to the registrar. I couldn't afford the time or the additional fees to do the job properly. That decision held me back professionally, but I had access to the intellectual world I cared about and slowly began writing a first book. Putting aside the Gothic humors of Yoknapatawpha County, I began thinking about comedy as a survival strategy among the Irish.

Survival was an issue in 1968 and 1969 when our campus was scorched by political protest. In that academic year a coalition of black and Puerto Rican faculty members and students brought charges of mismanagement against Joseph Mulholland, director of the program in which I was teaching for the second year. They seized control of the program while the Academic Senate, the governing body of the college, argued over the questions of how to proceed and specifically whether to allow Mulholland his legal right to answer the charges (which were later dropped).

Along with most of the faculty, I was ostracized by the coalition, though not by the students. When classes were disrupted, students continued with tutoring sessions and handed in papers. Despite the racial anger and confusion, they wanted to finish the semester. This is not the place for an analysis of the revolution that briefly shook Queens College. What I want to consider are some details that affected my thinking and propelled me along that bridge toward Manhattan.

Beginning with the first protests in December 1968 and continuing through the spring of 1969, the college went through a series of crises which had a grotesquely comic dimension. Our experience reflected the larger historical moment which joined the antiwar and civil rights movements. The Berrigan brothers, pacifist priests, were in jail, and on streets and campuses across the country minorities reached for power. In that climate the racial makeup of our program created a volatile situation. The majority of faculty and staff were white; the majority of students were black and Puerto Rican. Strikes throughout the university system and, particularly, the pressure exerted on City College in Harlem led to open admissions (anyone with a high school diploma could matriculate), a politically driven concession by college administrators. Chancellor Albert Bowker, who spoke enthusiastically about the changes, soon abandoned the City University for an appointment in California.

As the 1969 spring semester at Queens College unraveled, the white faculty were denounced by the coalition for "paternalism" and for being part of the "oppressive capitalist system." The latter was a familiar rhetorical tag which contained its grain of truth, though it was difficult to think of myself as an "oppressive capitalist" on eight thousand dollars a year. "Paternalism" was a charge meant to expose the colonial mentality of our enterprise. It suggested that, like certain nineteenth-century missionaries, we treated our students with condescension and encouraged dependency. This seemed to me exactly the reverse of everything the program was designed to do. Ironically, we probably helped to shape the new political consciousness. Along with Camus and Shakespeare, our students were reading James Baldwin, Eldridge Cleaver, Ralph Ellison, and Franz Fanon. They had returned the previous fall wearing dashikis, their hair billowing out in Afros. Despite what was happening, this struck me as a healthy thing, intellectually and psychologically validating, just as reading Maxine Hong Kingston or Virginia Woolf is validating to women.

The coalition was a different matter. This group wanted a bigger voice in what was essentially a program for minorities. But their tactics were scare tactics: escalating demands, physical intimidation, threats of turning the college into "another Hiroshima." Their actions had a deliberate theatrical dimension which attracted the media and frightened many on campus. Spectacles were staged. Speakers chanting "Black Power" disrupted classes, there were raids on the dining room and the library, windows were smashed, and equipment was broken. In a public voodoo ceremony on campus, effigies of the president and dean of faculty were skewered with pins. In this increasingly confrontational mode, the Puerto Ricans were overshadowed. After the first demonstrations the presence of a single black student wearing "shades" more than once caused people to scatter in fright. Quite a lesson for us all on the state of race relations in New York City.

Reinforcing the theatrical quality of the demonstrations were the costumes worn by the star performers. The tall African-American professor from Great Neck who acted as a mediator between the coalition and the college administration appeared at meetings in a dazzling white suit, African beads on his broad chest, sandals on his feet. His aide-de-camp, short and thin, was less resplendent despite a military cape. One of the more prominent leaders, who denounced remediation as "regressive," was a tall beautiful woman who wore brilliantly colored African garments. Appearing dramatically during a meeting of the Academic Senate, she hurled what looked like explosives into the assembly room and disappeared. Professors jumped to their feet and started running until they realized she had hurled small stink bombs.

To my Bronx working-class eye, the leaders appeared bizarre, though I was personally intimidated as well as anxious for students, some of whom had been physically threatened for supporting the director, Joe Mulholland. The only faculty member ever threatened, however, was an African-American, an old friend from Hunter who easily defended himself. The real pressure was on minority faculty, staff, and students. The rest of us were, in a sense, irrelevant. Along with a few colleagues, I met with the dean of faculty, a small, bitter man, to demand due process for Mulholland and to discuss ways of diffusing the crisis. The dean's response only confirmed the accusations of the coalition. "What do these people want?" he asked in low tones so we'd have to incline respectfully in his direction. "If it's just the degree, I'll be glad to certify them, to stamp B.A. or B.S. on their foreheads. Is that what they want?" It was the kind of cynicism that led to open admissions and a devalued degree. What was ostentatiously given with one hand was quietly taken away with the other.

Perhaps if there were no small children to worry about, I would have been bolder in speaking up myself. I don't know. I certainly wasn't experiencing "liberal guilt." The naked anger and aggression of racial confrontation was a shock. It had a visceral impact. People with whom I had shared meals and lessons met me now with blank stares. Three or four colleagues quit in disgust; most held on, hoping for a compromise solution.

Complicating the political scene at Queens College were sit-ins by Students for a Democratic Society (SDS) and a series of counterdemonstrations by conservative students furious at what they perceived as the conciliatory attitude of the administration. The SDS groups locked themselves in the upper floors of the thirteen-story tower normally inhabited by the administration and, when the elevators were subsequently immobilized, arranged for food supplies to be hauled up to them on ropes. They, too, had a flair for drama. For the most part, however, the coalition's tactics gave them the upper hand as well as the spotlight. At the most climactic point, our students marched onto the main campus shouting slogans and were met by angry white students who chased them back through the college gates. Before serious violence erupted, someone closed the gates between the two groups. A task force of very tough-looking policemen arrived on the scene, and the revolution melted away.

At the end of the semester the coalition retained control of the program, many students dropped out, and most of the white faculty were fired. Thereafter the power of the black and Puerto Rican leadership dwindled and, although the program continued, its relationship to the college was uneasy and increasingly submerged. With open admissions and the expansion of remedial courses at the college, its primary function was rendered obsolete. Relations within these academic communities festered for years. The number of African-American and Puerto Rican students dwindled (the opening of York College in nearby Jamaica had an impact), and Asian students took their place.

It seemed to me, in my disillusionment, that the demonstrators had revealed a terrible fault line in our society, which was scarcely repaired through open admissions. It was as though a Band-Aid were used to seal a mastectomy. I feared that this outbreak of violence would provide an excuse for doing less, not more, to improve the lot of poor minorities. For my own part I was angry and desperate after being fired. If I was complicit in a flawed system, I had worked hard for my students, many of whom did graduate from college. When I tried to return to teaching in Nassau County, I was targeted by my former principal as a "union activist" (mainly for picketing after school hours) and as a "radical" (for working with blacks and Puerto Ricans). It was hard to appreciate the catch-22 quality of the thing.

Luckily, before the summer was over, I was offered a job with the

English Department at Queens College. The chairman figured I probably knew something about the "nontraditional" students who would soon be appearing in their classes. But why me? There were plenty of good people to choose from. Of the nineteen who lost their jobs, two were rehired by the college, the only two with children. It turned out that Mulholland, who subsequently headed another innovative program at Fordham, had spoken on our behalf. This was the first time in my educational career that my own children were considered sympathetically.

Teaching basic courses for the next several years, I was stuck in a kind of professional limbo. Teaching was still a great pleasure, something inherently valuable in itself, though I missed the heady atmosphere of experimentation, of trying, however naïvely, to change the social system. My new students were fairly timid; few of them nurtured impossible dreams. When we were reading *Equus,* they thought that Peter Shaffer had got it right; at the average age of twenty, they regarded life around them as mainly humdrum. With an armload of books, there was plenty I could do to stir them up, open those eyes prematurely fogged by cataracts.

Actually, the main problem was not lack of status, but lack of money. Although I was working on the inside, so to speak, it was a struggle to pay the mortgage and keep the kids in sneakers. My upbringing as an Irish Catholic had stressed the unimportance of material things; the nuns and priests who influenced me had taken vows of poverty. With three degrees and two boys to support, I was still operating within that tradition. Perhaps this was a failure of initiative on my part; it can also be attributed to another convulsion of New York history.

In the 1970s the city was paralyzed by a major fiscal crisis, signaled by the infamous *Daily News* headline: "Ford to City: Drop Dead!" In 1976 our bankrupt university was forced to close, and professors in academic gowns lined up along with everybody else at unemployment offices. I won't say it was a humbling experience because there is a strong identification with the working class among CUNY faculty and staff. When we picketed that year at City Hall, we went in the company of hospital workers and clerks from municipal offices. I liked the feeling of solidarity and of taking political action, though in fact our gains were few. The university reopened, but some lost their jobs while the rest of us were stuck with small salaries and large classes.

Along with the surging tide of students, an opportunity to work in Irish studies materialized. The civil rights movement that began in Northern Ireland in 1967, inspired by Martin Luther King Jr., had come full circle. Reading about atrocities day after day, hearing of innocent people tortured and killed, Irish-Americans wanted to know more about their own roots. So I was drafted to provide interdisciplinary courses in Irish literature and history. This did not mean shutting myself into that ivory tower contemplated in the Bronx. Paradoxically, grappling with the history I thought I had left behind enabled me to grasp something larger.

Perhaps the best way to explain is by way of an incident that occurred in 1987 in Northern Ireland. That July I was driving through the green countryside of Tyrone after a few days on the coast of Donegal. I was hoping to reach Dublin by nightfall but didn't make it because of numerous checkpoints at which British soldiers with drawn guns inspected my car and driver's license. Exhaustion forced me to stay at a hotel in the border town of Omagh, where I was put through a more rigorous inspection. Guards, who were taking no chances with stray visitors, questioned my reasons for being there; the car was thoroughly searched and my description phoned to the desk clerk. The town itself, barricaded behind sandbags and barbed wire, was patrolled by soldiers. That night a local man, whose daughter had been shot the week before, was dragged from his bed and executed by the IRA.

The next morning I got in my car and drove away, but the memory of that town under siege is tenacious. It comes to mind when I read of some new atrocity in Kosovo or Sierra Leone. It gives me some understanding of the refugees from widely different cultures in Afghanistan, Ethiopia, Colombia, or Bangladesh who are drawn to Irish studies. Because of its long, terrible history, the Irish experience, as Edward Said has observed, can become a medium for confronting other people's memories of displacement. Some students now at Queens College have seen murder and rape at first hand; they have lost homes and possessions. Reading W. B. Yeats and Edna O'Brien, they are better able to articulate what they have been through themselves. Yeats's "rough beast" and O'Brien's "sacrificial women" have familiar features. Although their stories are far more horrific than my own, there are common strands that bring us together. We all carry baggage that still needs sorting out. I am not the only one who has lost a son.

Historians of Irish America typically speak of "progress." After all, John F. Kennedy got to be president. Irish names dot the list of top executives throughout corporate America. Unlike the starving, disease-ridden Irish who crowded into the ghettos of lower Manhattan 150 years ago, we're assimilated now. Some would argue that we've all become "white." I have a lot of trouble with this concept. It's important to retain a sense of vulnerability, to remember what we came from, however disturbing that is. Sometimes, indeed, it's necessary to double back. The past, as Faulkner so well understood, is never really past.

Highbridge itself was a kind of halfway station—a matter not simply of money or geography but of mind. Although a green flag sparkled in the doorway, my parents were enthusiastic about their new world. This gave me an edge in life which has not yet dulled even as I have come to recognize the imprint of poverty, revolution, and civil war. And the stories keep on coming; family memories are still entangled in Irish history, gapped, broken, inconclusive. Agnes and I were left with a strong sense of expectation unfulfilled, of ghosts to be exorcised. Only recently I learned that the famine victims of the 1840s buried at the Ruane farm in Mayo were children of an earlier generation. That's why one particular field, the Cúlán, was never plowed.

Our parents were stunned by history, and Mother never recovered. She was able to change her name but not the circumstances that crippled her, forced her as a child to work in the fields and to take menial jobs as an immigrant with little education. She raged at her limits, raged at us for escaping some of them. She took insult when none was intended; thought people laughed at her accent—like that of the old comical Bridget—when in fact they found it pleasing. Father had a greater capacity for humor, which widened his perspective, made him more flexible. Even when I divorced and remarried, breaking the rules of the Catholic Church, he wished me well. Ultimately, he came to terms with the place in which he found himself; Mother never did. At his funeral she wanted him remembered in song as a soldier wrapped in a green flag, brave and defiant as, of course, he had been.

I have written about the oscillating tone of family conversation, the

fusillade of wit that knocked us off balance. That oscillating quality determined our emotional balance as well. As children, Agnes and I were
urged to "step along, step along" and, at the same time, gripped posses-
sively, held to account. Perhaps, because of the undertow of Irish history,
one could say there is a parallel between our generation of Irish-Americans and the children of Holocaust survivors. There is a similar sense of
guilt and a religious intensity. We were not simply Roman Catholics but
Irish ones, with all the extremes of practice and belief the term implies.
How could we ever be good enough? Impelled toward professional
achievement, we were all the more conscious of our parents' deprivation
and sacrifice.

This struck me with brutal irony in January 1993 when Mother was
hospitalized in critical condition. Still pulled in two directions, I struggled to put her out of mind while we were desperately trying to find my
son. In the end she solved my dilemma in her own formidable way, refusing to die until spring.

Brian, at his brother's wedding, 1988. Courtesy of Photography by Fudge.

AT THE INTERIOR

Seaview, 1970

*I*n a photograph on the piano Brian, aged ten, stands on top of a broken willow tree, flexing his muscles. Triumphant in the aftermath of a tornado that ripped through Nassau County, taking a portion of our roof and smashing our willow against a neighbor's house. Immediately behind Brian rears up Finn MacCool, speckled red and white, the family cat.

Unlikely as it seems, we had picked that house because of the willow tree, the one feature that distinguished it from the row of small wood-and-brick ranch homes on either side. Lou Andreas-Salomé, lover of the poet Rilke and friend to Nietzsche and Freud, likened woman to the wandering snail, *die Schneckeli,* who carries her shelter around on her own back. In Salomé's theory this is woman's imaginative way of compensating for the loss of God, providing herself simultaneously with a sense of security and freedom from metaphysical and conventional moorings.

Moorings are essential to me. Each home we have inhabited is to some degree a compensation for one that has been lost, figuratively or otherwise. Each has necessitated some rebuilding, however modest, a deliberate act of repossession. The children and I moved to Seaview on a fierce hot day in August and set to work—Agnes and Father helping us—to steam off the hideous wallpaper. Everyone worked at the house, none of us particularly skilled, but all of us pleased with such a communal project. Even Mother decided to forgive me; she could resist neither the children nor the prospect of a garden. We planted the usual roses and tomatoes, my father staking them out as the vines grew, the boys trailing after him with hose and watering pail, liking the mud.

123

It was time to develop a feeling for the concrete. For building and painting and planting. For tackling every pot and pan and dish; scrubbing it, putting things in order. Amid the detritus of divorce, the prospect of a safer, happier life for my children took shape: a new house with a fanciful willow.

Seaview, 1972

I'm afraid to open the bedroom door because on the other side, waiting for me, is a fully grown Great Dane. The Hound of the Baskervilles. I can hear him snuffling; I can visualize the open jaw, the long, spindly legs, the capacity to jump for my throat. I've always been afraid of dogs. After ten minutes of shaky indecision, I take action. After all, this is my house. Why should I be cowering behind a door? Tiptoeing into the living room, I discover the beast curled up like a cat in the depths of a velvet armchair. But not for long. It's morning. The beast is wanting breakfast. So he pads after me into the kitchen, snuffling at the backs of my knees, nails clicking on the linoleum floor. Head up, he reaches my chest. He can look straight into Brian's eyes. Brian has brought him home for the weekend.

There is heated discussion in our household on the subject of dogs. The boys want one, naturally. Banjo is a compromise, one of several shaggy visitors that have arrived since Brian determined that a cat is not enough. Every boy needs a dog or a horse. But I remain firm. Smaller creatures are okay. I'll never have to walk them or pitch hay into their stalls.

That afternoon the boys have baseball practice while I have errands to run. What to do with Banjo, who prefers catching balls to waiting it out on the bench? Finally we lock him up in the basement with a bowl of creamy vittles. When we return two hours later, the creature has vanished, somehow managing to squeeze himself out through the tiny basement window. Where has he gone? Home is Manhattan, some twenty miles away. Even Lassie would have quailed at the prospect.

Then we see him in the distance, flying toward us. Those long, speckled legs hurling him forward with startling swiftness. He knocks Brian over in his joy and would have done the same to me had I not escaped into the garage. That evening we all go out for pizza—always the meal of choice. The boys sit next to me as I drive; Banjo sits in back, his head resting on the seatback between us, snuffling and drooling. Not yet a member of the family. But close.

Seaview, 1974

On an ordinary Thursday afternoon in May, I am waiting for Brian to come home from school. Lee was here a half hour ago, changed into his track suit, and is already out running his three miles. Another half hour goes by, and I decide to walk down to the junior high. When I don't see him among the kids on the front steps or in the small crowd around the soccer field, I head for the principal's office, where I learn that Brian hasn't been in school all day. In fact, he has been missing several classes lately, although no one has informed me of this before now. Don't panic! I begin checking the homes of his friends. Lee goes out on his bike to look. Eventually we take the car and drive back and forth through the neighborhood, stopping at the Pizza Hut, at McDonald's, combing through the arboretum on the town border. We can't find him.

Now I am afraid. Yet I hesitate to call the police. Where was he those other days? We live near Jones Beach, a great attraction in this fine sunny weather. Perhaps he's there with friends. But no one else seems to be missing; no one seems to know anything about it.

Then the phone call comes from Hackensack, New Jersey. Lee and I drive at maddeningly slow speed through rush hour traffic, and eventually find him after nightfall in a bowling alley in the dreariest part of this very dreary town.

He has no particular explanation. He started out hitchhiking and got this far, bought himself a hamburger, bowled a few games, and ran out of money. He doesn't understand why we're so upset. In the gloomy light he looks small and thin, younger than his fourteen years, much younger than the tough-looking kids around the pinball machine. He has no sense of danger whatsoever.

So it begins. A different kind of rebellion. There are consultations with teachers, therapists; even the school superintendent steps in. Brian is tutored at home; he attends two private schools. Nothing works for long.

He is slipping away. He cannot or will not talk about his problems, though he is an intelligent, articulate boy, who later on will regale us with stories just as his grandfather did. Only his stories conceal and evade whatever is tormenting him.

Seaview, 1975

A police call late at night: They are holding Brian. Nothing can be done until the next day.

We have no lawyer, and there's no time to find one. It's a Monday morning after a long, crowded weekend. The prisoners, women and men, black and white, look bad as they're led into the courtroom in pairs. My son, dirty, bedraggled, is handcuffed to a heavyset older man accused of armed robbery. When he turns to face the judge, I see that the seat of his jeans has been torn away. He stands there angry, lines of exhaustion etched on his face, his tattered backside to the packed court.

He will be held until bail is posted—two thousand dollars. When I go to see him that afternoon, I haven't yet managed to raise the money, but I have found a lawyer. He tells me not to worry. He didn't do it. The prisoners are behind narrow, barred windows. Sealed in. The visitors facing them are on stools in a narrow corridor. All communication is by phone. Brian's face is very small, very thin, very fragile. He wears a faded blue shirt and fresh jeans. No visible stripes. He smokes incessantly, so I promise to bring more cigarettes. He can't eat, can't sleep. He's been up all night, going through interrogation. The police, he tells me, were pretty rough. Now he's being held separately in a special cell because he's just sixteen. Nothing to do but look at the walls, wait for release.

The stories are all true. The bars clang. The corridors are long and narrow and grey. The people behind the bars look much the same as those of us looking in.

A lone woman had stopped her car at a red light two blocks from our house. It was nine o'clock at night. Brian, waiting at the intersection, reached into the car demanding her purse, which contained twelve dollars. He said he had a knife in his pocket, and he did. Within ten minutes he was caught by the police as he sat on the curbside, the purse still in his hands. He was smoking marijuana, one of the many drugs then seeping into suburbia.

He has no record, so he is placed on parole, the felony charge suspended if he abides by the rules for two years. But he doesn't abide by rules. He slips away to the beaches of Florida, the redwood forests of California. He figures it will all blow over in time, but it never does.

New Paltz, 1980

The front page of the *Times* catches my eye although I don't make the connection immediately. "Storms batter California. Heavy flooding in Ben Lomond. Houses washed away on Route 9."

For the past two years Brian has been living in Ben Lomond, a community with a lively interest in Scottish rituals, music, and games. I have visited him there. "Surprised, aren't you?" he said, with a grin. The log house was large and comfortable. There were paintings and sketches on the wall, some of them his own. Brian invited me into the kitchen where he was cooking spaghetti, while keeping an eye on a two-year-old girl, the youngest member of the household. On his head was a black sombrero, which was never removed while he worked away at kitchen chores, cutting up onions, setting the table. The baby played with his boots whenever he settled down. He told some amusing stories that day about raccoons they were raising and how quickly they found their way into the refrigerator and about the trout in their backyard creek. The trout was discovered when they were cleaning out a fish tank and had temporarily lodged their angelfish in a pool formed at the bend of the creek. That's when the trout appeared, swallowing every tiny fish. They never managed to catch him. He was too shrewd.

After reading those headlines, I call Ben Lomond repeatedly that day and the day that follows. Telephone lines are down, but messages are being taken by the Red Cross. There is no word until late the second day when the phone rings. Brian has hiked for six miles out of the disaster area to get supplies and to call us. The house and all his friends are safe, though neighbors have lost everything. He is going back to join the rescue work. It is a fine moment in his life, a redeeming moment as he tells it, battling his way through wind and rain, torrents of mud and debris, to call home and then return along the same disaster-strewn route to bring food, help, the benefit of his energy and good will.

That was Brian at his best. The man in the gap.

New Paltz, 1983

A postcard from New Orleans dated June 6. Brian has rejoined the company of bikers, old-time hippies, hustlers, Vietnam vets, men and women who move around a lot. Who work steadily for a year or two and then the itch comes, somebody presses too hard, and it's time to go somewhere else. There are networks out there, communes, safe houses, where they crash for a time, get their bearings, get laid, and get high. In summer they camp out; in winter they go south or west to California, nestling into log cabins up in the Santa Cruz Mountains. They're fond of sports and rock concerts; they watch television. No doubt there's more, but we never hear about that directly. Brian's stories are tinged with romance. He sees himself as a rugged individualist, an adventurer who's just missed the last wagon train. He has reconstructed himself along American lines, but he is one of the traveling people.

He comes in telling tales, feeding our dream of a good life for him. We catch him in our nets, draw him back into the family. He is all we could wish, for a month or two. Good-natured, witty, handy with tools, making his way as a carpenter. He even likes to cook, serving up cauldrons of spaghetti, carving up the roast beef. "It's so nice to be home."

At times he arrives on our doorstep with a small caravan in tow. An assortment of pals, male and female; an enormous dog, part Doberman, part Great Dane; a small, handicapped, very intelligent child. They set up camp in our living room. Roll out their blankets and sleeping bags. In exchange for food, they provide more stories, all of them trained on the past. You can see how practiced they are. Hardly a dull moment in their lives. They stretch out with deeply ingrained patience, having little of the ordinary sense of time. There is no particular plan in mind, no schedule to meet. They "go with the flow."

Brian has a snake story, several of them in fact. This one takes place in the Great Smoky Mountains of Tennessee.

There was a call for help from somebody's tough old grandmother. "Was it Billy Bones?" (Everyone has a distinctive name. Brian calls himself Stock, short for Woodstock; his friend Jack is called Dog). Anyway this old grandmother could handle a rifle like John Wayne. Feisty, a good shot, but outnumbered. So the posse moves in to back her up, make sure they don't push her off the land. She feeds them grits and hot coffee, and they decide to have a look around the territory. Where they come across a gathering of snake worshipers. The minister sits in the middle holding two enormous rattlesnakes. Other snakes are being passed around. The minister thrusts the two snakes together, but instead of biting each other they sink those deadly fangs into him. Brian intervenes, knowing something about snakes. The minister waves him off—no interference from outsiders—and the circle of the faithful gathers round. Brian calls the state troopers, but by the time they arrive the man is dead. They shoot the snakes one by one.

The index finger of Brian's right hand appears partly gnawed off—the result of a rattler bite when he was hitchhiking through Colorado last summer. Like the scar over his right eye and the tattoos on both heavily muscled arms, it marks him as an experienced man, an adventuring man. One who has little to do with the straight world of the nine-to-five propertied classes.

He's happiest on a bike or in an old pickup truck driving through open space, watching the landscape reel away in front of him, but never so totally absorbed in wind and weather that he fails to spot the whirling red eye of a patrol car on the horizon. He is vigilant in his determination of freedom. There are all kinds ready to close in, tie him up, and tie him down. I'm not speaking about young women, though there are plenty of them as well, pleasant and pretty, from pious and seemingly normal homes. They've stayed with us, too. Smoking and talking incessantly about Mom and Dad, bivouacked in our spare room.

The fact is I'm not sure who Brian is anymore, though I've consulted the usual specialists, who've provided the usual theories. He seems to know me far better than I know him. His stories are intended to soothe, cajole, tell us what we want to hear. He knows how desperately I love him, but the flow of words, jokes, tall tales, drowns me out. He promises everything, dutifully visiting aunts and cousins, congenial to a fault. Then he breaks it off, leaves as suddenly as he arrived, always on a note of breakdown, misunderstanding, a bruise to remember him by.

We have different obsessions. While he travels the peaks and valleys of Montana, Wyoming, Alaska, I move along a narrow trajectory from the Upper West Side of Manhattan to Queens College, to the mountains in upstate New York. There's little chance of arson or a bulldozer wrecking the landscape here. As I keep digging in, trying to recover what's been lost, does Brian keep moving in a kindred dream, expecting to find it all out there somewhere, that visionary America that won't go to pieces or break your heart?

New Paltz, 1992

My heart is unsteady. Even in the Shawangunk Mountains on days of relative calm, it stirs unpredictably, leaving me giddy, dislocated, dropping into a kind of abyss in which the extremities are numbed. I don't quite know what's there at my fingertips. I rarely lose consciousness, but experience a kind of free fall from my perceptual perch, so to speak. There's an erratic, quick, additional beat to this preposterous muscle, a compensatory motion to balance a mitral valve that doesn't close properly. I've seen the electronic shadow on a sonogram; it reminds me of the whistle on old wood-burning locomotives, a flimsy apparatus but piercingly effective in alarm. In the Western films I loved as a child it was sounded at the precise moment when the engineer spotted the washed-out bridge or the felled tree dead ahead.

Hollis, Queens, 1992

February. Mother has had another stroke. She lies in bed most of the day now, badly crippled, but talking on inexhaustibly as before. She cannot always locate the present or determine what is happening or where she is. This doesn't stop her from putting events together in her own ineluctable fashion. She drifts through the Cúlán, Tor an Chor, Cnoc an Phortaigh, the familiar fields of Mayo. She observes that the air is filled with golden specks, a shower of them. The boundaries between sleeping and waking are less and less certain. She talks to her sisters as children and to her mother, long dead. And then ambushes me abruptly: "Where is your father? . . . He hasn't been in since Sunday. . . . Why hasn't he called or at least written? . . . Maybe something has happened." She suspects me of withholding information, believing that he's around somewhere and, if she can just hit on the right question, she will find him. So she persists. "Is he coming over for dinner? . . . Why don't you give him a call?" When she hears yet again that he has died, she weeps with fresh bitterness. Over and over.

And indeed, why can't I call him up? The idea doesn't seem altogether implausible, given our mutual grief, our mutual state of mind. When I was in Dublin two years ago, I was obsessed with the idea that if I walked along the Liffey as far as the Four Courts, he would be there.

A great and terrible change has come over her. She is frail and thin, her belly grotesquely swollen, her bones prominent beneath the skin. The skin is translucent; arms and legs seem almost without flesh. But her face is silvery and beautiful, framed in soft, thickening white hair.

Last summer her features were so distorted with fury at finding herself partially disabled that her eyes seemed oddly misaligned. He skin was mottled, her lips compressed on the word "No!" What enraged her most, her vanity undimmed, was her own reflection in the mirror. Now she has become humorous and makes little jests with the women who look after her, whom last summer she would have battered with her cane.

April. "What has happened to me?" She is more and more weary. "When will it end?" She has little faith in doctors ("What do they know?") or, it seems, in anything else. All her life an ardent churchgoer, she is polite to the deacon on Sunday morning but curiously indifferent to his prayers. She talks to the dead directly, no longer needing any intermediary.

I try reading stories aloud, and she listens patiently before interrupting—slyly—with a request for tea. I try a poem translated from the Irish, thinking that might amuse her:

"O Woman of Three Cows, agra! Don't let your tongue thus rattle!" She startles us both by furnishing the lines:

O don't be a saucy, don't be stiff, because you may have cattle.
That tongue of yours wags more than charity allows
Don't be saucy, don't be stiff because you may have cows.

May. The foot as trope: Just to keep her company, I am crippled myself, one rickety ankle sprained yet again on the eve of my older son's wedding. I danced at the wedding and hiked afterwards around Mount Rainier, Marianne Moore's "octopus of ice," building up scar tissue that finally bound the nerve. Now this last, long year of Mother's life, I can scarcely walk at all. It will heal in time, but it has not improved my character nor inspired other modes of operation. The Irish need to walk, however shaky their feet, however uncertain the territory. I share her tedium.

July. Mother is telling people that I am dead. She weeps for me, confusing me perhaps with her sister Margaret. Or is it her fear that I am secretly ill and won't tell her? Or her realization that she herself is dying? The maintenance man telephones my office: She has told him she is being kidnapped, accusing her nurse. Her real self has been taken away. She is trapped, bewildered; she doesn't even understand how very trapped she is. She looks at me steadily, framing a new question: "How do you think your father feels now that he's gone?"

September. She can barely talk now. Leaning back on her pillow, utterly helpless, she smiles: "Poor Maureen." Her face, wreathed in oddly thick white hair, is smooth, gaunt, masklike. Her eyes, released for a few days from the fog of pneumonia, are a luminous blue. She nods graciously at the visiting nurse: "How kind of you to come." After quarreling bitterly all last year, she offers me peace. Inside all the shapes she has worn was this final shape.

New Paltz, 1995

Grief strips away the calluses of experience which dull the senses and protect the mind. Here in New Paltz we are surrounded by trees, wonderful dark hulks outlined against the snow. The emptiness, the sense of absence presses itself against the trees. Brian was an avid climber. He scaled our largest hemlock, over eighty feet tall, to saw off the crown, severely damaged by lightning. He scaled that hemlock effortlessly, or at least his climbing seemed effortless, so rapidly and surely he ascended. I keep expecting him to materialize in the branches. Like Sweeney in the trees, perhaps.

I keep company with ghosts. I can visualize Mother quite easily, and what is uppermost is her curiosity. I wish I could tell her things. True, not everything, but she liked to know what I was writing as well as the domestic news, the garden, the children. For ten years I didn't have a husband to share this with, so I shared it with my parents and, of course, with Agnes, much more as time went on. When I think of Mother now, or when she almost appears, she is full of questions. What has she missed? She is keen on offering advice in her prickly, willful manner. Such certitude. Such optimism.

Brian comes with a different set of questions, very insistent, interposing himself now between me and the pages on which I write. He appears to be in his early twenties, vigorous, intense. His is not a tragic face, but a baffled one. "Why?" he asks. And again "why?" Then the face changes, and I imagine other things he might be saying. Sometimes I imagine chagrin. He didn't expect to die.

There is a way, in time, that one possesses the dead, particularly the beloved dead. They are placed in certain attitudes; one comes to certain conclusions about them. I think of dear friends this way. There is a raw sense of loss, of life cut off too soon, that is still, after years, fresh in mind. They have become bright points on my compass. I steer by their light, their intelligence, and courage. And my father was such a point. Until Brian's death, he was a resource summoned up at will, an amused, benevolent presence.

On a visit this year, Nancy brings an album of photos of her life with Brian, many of them taken in New Hampshire in 1989, 1990, and 1991. Here he is with their son, Jeremiah, on hands and knees in a jumble of Christmas presents and, again, standing on a rocky shelf at the foot of the White Mountains, arms stretched out, taking it all in. Here they are together, swathed in plastic bags, eyes concealed behind wind goggles, grinning goofily through a summer downpour. While I think too often of what didn't work out, she reminds me of much that did.

New Paltz, 1999

There was another young man, Christopher McCandless, who, after graduating from college and thus pleasing his parents, set out to explore the American West and Southwest. Giving away most of his property, working at odd jobs for food, he determined that he could survive alone in the extreme conditions of the Mohave Desert. In April 1992 he headed for the Alaskan frontier, toting books by Jack London, Henry David Thoreau, and John Muir. Six months later his emaciated body was found north of Mount McKinley in an abandoned school bus. Mere pathos? The writer Jon Krakauer, who pieced together the details of McCandless's journey, comes to a different conclusion, reminding us how dissatisfying a conventional life seems to idealistic or rebellious or vivacious young people. And for young men of a certain cast of mind, the American wilderness continues to exert a profound attraction. When he was twenty-five, Krakauer himself nearly perished climbing a hazardous Alaskan peak known as the Devil's Thumb. He argues that such risk taking is not simply aberrant behavior but is genetically programmed in our species. Those who survive, like himself or Muir, the conservationist, are admired for their courage and venturesome spirit. Krakauer speculates that some men need to invent a difficult ritual passage to manhood.*

Nothing in Brian's life that I am aware of was as dangerous as the Devil's Thumb or the Alaskan wilderness. But it seems to me that he was engaged in a similar rite of passage by living outside the safe harbor of custom and time clocks. When he was seventeen, eighteen, and nineteen, he camped out winter and summer, fishing for food and hunting wild game. He had the family stubbornness as well as a fierce will to independence. He worked as a carpenter but also as a lumberjack, a fisherman, and a firefighter. Fond of pine wood and pure mountain air, he repaired roofs and high-voltage wires. He liked working, "keeping busy," but enjoyed the extra spark that came from dangerous work. In November 1992 he was in Florida repairing buildings damaged by the hurricane. The first roof he was sent to survey collapsed under him, damaging his ribs and who knows what else. He refused a doctor. Those injuries had not healed when he went out by himself on New Year's Eve.

Into the Wild. New York: Villard (1996).

So I speculate about the last hours of Brian's life, wondering what kind of pain prompted the fatal mix of drugs and alcohol. It still doesn't make sense to me. It never will.

"It is those we live with and love and should know who elude us." Norman Maclean, who wrote those words, liked to remember his brother—another bright spirit who died young—fishing for trout in the Big Blackfoot River in Montana.

I will remember Brian arriving unexpectedly in New Paltz, bringing his carpentry tools or lobsters from Maine. Ready to start cooking, doing odd jobs around the house, mending in our lives whatever he could. It was in some ways a kind of game we played back and forth. He would not take from us what we wanted most to give. But he recognized our eagerness to give it, by reciprocating, humorously, in kind.

These days there is much talk of closure, of rituals that enable one to accept death and put an end to grieving. Writing a book or contributing to a worthy cause might enable one to do that. But I don't believe in closure, though focusing on loss can turn the heart into a small, bitter thing. There is, after all, an alternative. Let us call it openness.

When his brother died in the Irish Revolution, Father became a medical corpsman, doing what he could to aid the wounded. Years later he saved a neighbor's young child from choking to death with diphtheria. He gave her mouth-to-mouth resuscitation without considering the risk to himself. The story reverberated through the apartment house, east of the Concourse, where we lived then. Our father had saved a child's life. No wonder we trusted him. While his actions didn't truly offset the losses he had experienced, there was a sense of recuperation because he remained open to that possibility. It was not only sorrow he carried across the Atlantic. When tragedy moved toward him again, he was ready to meet it.

I take it as a good sign that at last I'm beginning to walk without a cane or crutches. Not, of course, with my old energy and momentum, but with a surer sense of the landscape I think of as home.

Tomorrow is New Year's Eve, *an beama bail* the Irish term it, the "dangerous cusp" of the year. Wherever you are, Brian, may there be light and peace always.

He climbed the hemlock near the top,
Where lightning had blighted and left it white,
Carrying the old saw, loose in its handle,
And hung on with one hand, his ledge
A high thin branch.
Then, cutting into the dead mast,
He shouted to his mother, who stood
On the deck of the house adrift
In groundwaters rising with all the rain.
"Come down," she called. Was she loud
Enough to be heard?
"Watch out below!"
The red beard turned gold above the shade.

A surge of sturdy thrusts. He stopped,
And, clinging to the bare trunk,
Dropped the saw. The blade
Hit rock, shot free.
Steadying himself with both hands,
While we, not wanting to,
Watched, he lowered one foot
Onto another dead branch
Carefully, and then, testing,
Let both boots rest there,
Before he turned around
To take the next step down,
Stretched his left leg until he reached
At last the lowest
Rung in the gaping ladder of boughs,
And leapt.

Later that summer morning
He patched our steep roof.
We never mentioned the hemlock.

The tall bare top has lowered there,
Hanging on by the few inches he left unsawed.
Laying its shadow across glass panels and doors,
Long since he went away,
Leaving us silence for years
Before he left the earth.

David Kleinbard
"Anniversary"

APPENDIX

APPENDIX

Sligo, 1919–1922

*T*he following is excerpted from recollections set down by my father, Daniel Waters, in the 1970s and left to me after his death in 1983. I am including it here to illustrate the power of those Irish memories that were firmly impressed on me as a child and helped to shape my own view of the world.

The Waters family had a farm in Cloonelly, which is situated under Ben Bulben, near Drumcliff—Yeats country; they were tenants of the Gore-Booths at Lissadell for generations. Though it escaped the extensive damage suffered in Cork city, this beautiful land of Innisfree was hit hard by guerrilla warfare between 1919 and 1921. Police were ambushed and killed. British irregulars terrorized families and burned their homes. Like many of the young men in the area, my father, at sixteen, was drawn into the fighting despite reservations. After the truce in 1921, he joined the Free State Army, serving first in an artillery unit that shelled the Four Courts and afterwards as a medic. In 1924—something I discovered after his death and cannot account for—be took part in the army mutiny. His brother, Michael, an ardent Republican, died at the age of seventeen in a futile attempt to place a mine inside a barracks occupied by the British. A younger sister also died as a result of war.

A question that troubled my father all his life was why he had survived instead of the others. His account emphasizes the element of chance. Many he knew personally died because of faulty ammunition, misunderstandings, the general confusion and hostility of the times. At one point in the civil war he was himself nearly shot, when he ran into a company of Irish speakers from Galway and was forced at gunpoint to explain himself in Irish. Certainly an ironic episode in the linguistic history of the nation.

My father started out as a romantic idealist, planting the tricolor on Ben Bulben after the Rising of 1916 and carrying messages for the Volunteers. But the events of 1919–1923 were disillusioning. War also widened his perspective, freed him from farm life, and led him to emigrate to America.

The first of the trouble started over the land. In the parish of Cliffony, which was the seat of the Bishop, there was a Father Michael Flannagan who was vice president of Sinn Féin [the nationalist party] and a real radical. He later was defrocked. At that time the people of the community wanted the estates of the absent landlords cut up and divided among the small farmers and the landless classes. This had the full support of Father Michael. Every Sunday he would preach on the evils of the absentee system.

Now, the local police were stationed across the road from the church, and the sergeant and five men attended Mass regularly, occupying the first row of seats. The sergeant, whose name was Perry, called on Father Michael to lay off the agitating or he would have to take action. Father Michael responded the next Sunday by calling on the police to resign. Sergeant Perry took out his notebook and took down everything, thereby signing his own death warrant. Up to that time no serious action had been taken against the RIC [Royal Irish Constabulary, the local police] in that part of Sligo.

In the far end of the territory there was a man named Jordan who owned a public house and was pro-British. He was not a spy in the true sense of the word, but when the local police were around, he was always calling for their help in minor matters. The Volunteers cut the shafts out of his cart at night, and in the morning when he found it, he sent a messenger to Cliffony to notify the police. The IRA [Irish Republican Army] in the meantime set up an ambush on the hill of Grange about one-half mile from the village and called in the flying column. This column was made up of men from outside the community. They were to show themselves at their regular occupations on the day of the ambush so that, when the military investigated, they could claim they were at their usual tasks. That is why my brother from B Company [he and his brother belonged to different companies of the Third Western Division of the IRA] knew all about it and was posted to direct the column to the retreat direction after the ambush while I, who belonged to A Company in whose territory it took place, did not know anything.

Sergeant Perry and five men answered the call that morning of October 1920. Based on testimony of the man left behind to take care of the barracks, who himself was killed a few months later, most of the men considered it a dangerous mission and were afraid they were being set up. But Perry asked, were they not members of His Majesty's forces, and when were they afraid to go on established rounds? So they started off on their bikes fully armed, and when they reached the top of the hill of Grange, they were called on to surrender. Perry jumped from his bike and called to his men to open fire. In that moment he was shot through the mouth and heart and died instantly. Four of his men died at the same time; the fifth, badly wounded, cycled down the hill and then fell off his bike. The leader of the column and three others caught up to him. One of the men tried to kill him, and the leader of the column had to disarm him. This was the testimony given by the wounded constable, Clark, at the inquest held some time later.

This ambush took place at eleven–thirty and was over by twelve. It was a nice warm day. My brother, Michael, and I were digging potatoes for a man by the name of Gilmartin who had two sons in the RIC, and we heard the shots. Michael said he had to get some bags for the potatoes but did not come back for over two hours. He had the bags and also the news that the police were ambushed. That was all he said. If you went through those days, you knew the less you said, the less you could be accounted for.

About seven o'clock when it was getting dark, the Black and Tans and the Auxiliary [British irregulars who were much feared and hated] arrived at Grange to pick up the bodies of the dead police. The Auxiliaries started to drink anything they could get their hands on. Then they lined up all the people of Grange and started to beat them, trying to find out who was in the ambush and the names of the local Volunteers. Any house where the men were not home they burned to the ground. And when they found some young men, they beat them unmercifully. From that time on no one slept very sound as raids were carried on once a week at about five o'clock in the morning. We knew by the speed of the lorries if they were Auxiliary, and we went into hiding at a safe distance and waited until we got the all clear. On the other hand when the soldiers and police started a roundup, they came at an easy pace, and we took our chance. That is, all of us that were not on the run. I must say they did not discriminate. They rounded up the young and old, supporters of the crown and nonsupporters alike.

What we did enjoy was having them round up an old salty character whose name was Patrick Foran. He lived alone and was a bit hard of hearing. The Tans had to smash the door down before he heard them, and then he came out fighting. I must say he was not afraid of anything. He was about seventy years old and had served in the British and American armies.

The military generally held us for about four hours, and then if there were trenches to be filled, they picked out twenty of us and took us along. When they got near the job, they just slowed down and made us jump from the lorries. We suffered a few bruises. An old soldier showed me how to relax as I jumped, and I must say it worked then and after in some falls. So something good comes from every experience. When we had the job finished, they lectured us on the folly of doing anything to help the IRA, and we were back that night and opened the trenches.

We called the Auxiliary "the destroying angels." They would tell you to make a run for it as you knew the ground and had a good chance to get away. To offset this the mothers, wives, and sisters followed at a distance. This helped to keep them in line. The women of Ireland got little recognition for their part in the war for independence except for a few that did a lot of shouting and little else for the cause. All mothers that had sons in the IRA realized, when they joined, they were in for the duration as anyone in the ranks knew what the setup was, the names of the leaders, and the location of arms dumps. I do not know of anyone that defected, but there were reports that some did and were found dead under peculiar circumstances. The deaths were blamed on the British as it would be bad publicity for the IRA if it was known that they executed members who were not fit to live up to the conditions they had to endure.

While the Auxiliaries were burning the houses after the Grange ambush, we were preparing an ambush on the Auxiliaries between Castlegarron and Drumcliff. We worked all night digging trenches along the road the lorries had to pass through and cutting the fences to give the IRA a direct line of fire and a retreat line if the Auxiliary approached from the wrong direction. We also planted a mine. We did our job well and finished at six o'clock in the morning, cold and hungry. We then had to march five miles to be out of range of a roundup. But nothing happened. The arms did not arrive the night before the planned ambush. The Brigadier General William Devins, the Brigade Intelligence Officer Kilbride, and Brigade Adjunct Conway were captured by the Black and Tans near Ballysadare transporting the guns from the police killed in the Grange ambush in an open car. Needless to remark, the Tans went to work on them, and when they were through, they had to be taken to Sligo General Hospital where they were held without visitor rights for three months and then imprisoned in England. These events paralyzed the IRA in North Sligo for a time....

We continued drilling twice a week at different places and attended lectures and Irish dances, and of course the dances were better attended than the lectures. We had plays once a month in the Temperance Hall in Grange. These were patriotic plays with Robert Emmet, Wolfe Tone, and Patrick Sarsfield to encourage desire for a free and independent Ireland. We did not get much in the way of guns. We drilled with wooden guns. I did see a selection of shotguns and a few revolvers. That was all besides a few homemade bombs and a mills bomb that we used for practice with the detonator removed....

In 1921 there was one policeman in particular who did his best to jail or kill every member of the IRA; his name was Kelly. He did his job so well he was promoted to sergeant himself along with one other, whose name I have forgotten. They were notified to come to Dublin headquarters for their stripes and acclaim for their good works. In the meantime the IRA declared the death sentence on them. On their way back from Dublin, they were taken off the train at Ballysadare and shot. Sergeant Kelly was entombed in Drumcliff cemetery across from where Yeats is buried. That night the IRA came and planted a mine that blew the casket out of the grave and across the wall of the cemetery.

The day they were shot, I and two more young fellows drove a herd of twenty-four cattle ten miles to Sligo. The pay was ten shillings each, and we earned it. When we delivered the cattle, I bought tobacco for Dennis Watters (no relation at the time), who had been imprisoned in the Cranmore jail. What I did not know was that the Black and Tans had taken over the jail as their headquarters; most of the prisoners were sent to Belfast. Anyway I called on one of the Tans to let me in. He opened the door of a room that was pretty dark after coming in out of the sunlight. He said, "Wait in there," and locked the door. When my eyes grew accustomed to the darkness, I realized I was in the room alone with the two dead policemen, and they were covered with blood. I was only sixteen years old. I am afraid I was in deep shock and, as I did not cry out, they kept me there for about an hour.

They then took me out and questioned me. "Where were you at eleven a.m.? Did you shoot the two police? Do you know who did it? Who is your commander, and what brought you to the jail to see a murderer?" He meant Dennis. I told them the truth as far as I was concerned. I did not know anything about the episode. They asked me did I know Sergeant Kelly, and did I want him dead? When I said I knew him and had no opinion about him, they cuffed me around for a while. Then Sergeant Connolly came on the scene and told them I was a good boy and a widow's son, and they let me go. [Note: Sergeant Connolly of the RIC saved a number of local men from serious injury; according to my father, "he was never interfered with and retired to Belfast after the war."]

As one might expect under martial law, the innocent as well as the not-so-innocent were swept into jail, Dennis Watters among them. His experience reveals a good deal about the temper of the time. He was imprisoned because of a chance remark by my father, who was probably thinking of his own prospects at that point. This unfortunate incident originated in the 1919 rent strike and the use of process servers against resisting landholders. The IRA responded by threatening the process servers and burning their papers. A local man, Thomas Walker, was raided twice and, when he refused to cooperate, was finally executed by the IRA. Before dying he turned in a list of twenty names, including my father's and Dennis Watters's.

The memoir continues:

I'm afraid it was my fault Dennis was sentenced to death for the murder of Thomas Walker. At the time Walker was raided, Dennis's mother and father had just died, and I was his substitute, carrying the mail from Breaghey post office, when I met Thomas Walker on the road. As he was old and, I think, nearsighted, as well as a bit drunk at the time, he threatened me. He would have the handcuffs on me before the night was out. With me it was a joke. I replied, "You might be dead before the night is out." He went home and made out a statement to the effect that the mailman threatened him with death, and his son swore he identified Dennis during the raid by the way he held his shoulders. I know Dennis never took any part in raiding or shooting. But if you were charged with a crime, and you were a member of the IRA or a supporter, you did not recognize the court, so it was easy for them to pass judgment on you. Dennis was a great believer in [Eamon] De Valera [leader of the antitreaty forces] until he joined the new government. I used to kid him about Michael Collins saving his neck. [My father's neck was saved by the intervention of Sergeant Connolly.]

Among those imprisoned from Castlegarron was Patrick Farrell, Brigade Intelligence Officer. It was his duty to check on all reports on spies, and he strongly opposed the execution of Thomas Walker. He said he was harmless and the butt of jokes. He was overruled and took no part in what followed. Two others had served in the British army in France for two years. They had no political affiliation. Most of them did ten months in Belfast jail and two, including Dennis, were saved from the hangman by the truce [engineered by Michael Collins]. They were also looking for my brother, Michael, who had just died. We did not make known to them that he was buried as they would want an inquest. These were among the greatest hardships of the fight for independence....

In 1921 came the truce, and we were called on to parade to meet the released prisoners. We were growing weary of all the demands that were made. We had to take care of the families of those that were in prison. The crops had to be put in and harvested. I must say we did not have any spare time. "A" Company fell in at eight o'clock in the morning at the Grange Hall. Now that there was no more fighting, Volunteers were coming out of the woodwork. The parade was poorly planned. Most of the prisoners were coming from Belfast and Dublin, and the English with their usual cunning released them late in the day so they did not arrive until after dark. We marched six miles to meet them. We were young and had good appetites, so when we got the order to fall out with no plans for food, we were a very downcast lot of marchers. The priests had a lot more pep. The prisoners were taken in hand by the Green Cross, who wined and dined them. The band played and the politicians made their speeches, welcoming them home and saying what they would do for them when Ireland was free. Maybe they believed themselves that there was a pot of gold at the end of the rainbow, but alas the dreams came to an end too soon.

In a few months everything was upside down, and the scramble for positions was on again. The rule of the IRA was that when an officer above the rank of section commander went to prison, his position had to be filled from the ranks. On their release from prison, these officers found their positions filled with younger men with no order for them to revert to their old rank. What you had then was all chiefs, no braves, hence the smashup.

In 1922 the Black and Tans and the Auxiliary were recalled to England, and there was great rejoicing through the length and breadth of Ireland by the supporters of the Volunteers. On the other hand, you had the supporters of the British forces, particularly the merchants, who supplied the forces of the crown. It was a big blow to the economy. The people of Sligo town were pro-British but, while they did not like the way things were going, they wanted law and order and strongly supported the Free State. I firmly believe if it had ever come to a vote, they would have wanted the British back as there was a lot of British money flowing into Sligo to the widows of soldiers killed in World War I and to disabled soldiers and sailors. They sure supported the crown in World War I....

In February 1922 we arrived in Dublin 150 strong and took over from the British army. We had months of training for the part we had to play in exchanging the guard, but our uniforms were a mixed lot, and many Dubliners gave us the Bronx cheer, especially the ladies of the night, who were making a living off the British forces. Also the pub owners as there was a lot of temperance in the Volunteers. In March we proceeded to Athlone Custom Barracks and took over from the King's Own Regiment. We entered a new way of life, a way of life that a lot of us did not understand.

Well I remember our first day in Athlone as regular soldiers of the Free State. Captain Clancy was still in charge of our group, and he asked for a volunteer who knew how to handle a rifle. A man by the name of Emmet stepped forward. He was an ex-British soldier and should have known the score, but he loaded his rifle and started to demonstrate. When he unloaded, there was still one round up the breech. He pulled the trigger, the gun discharged and killed a soldier on the other side of the room. We went on guard duty that night with empty rifles. Emmet was placed under arrest, given six months of hard labor and a dishonorable discharge. The captain was reprimanded. That was a poor beginning for the life we thought we would love.